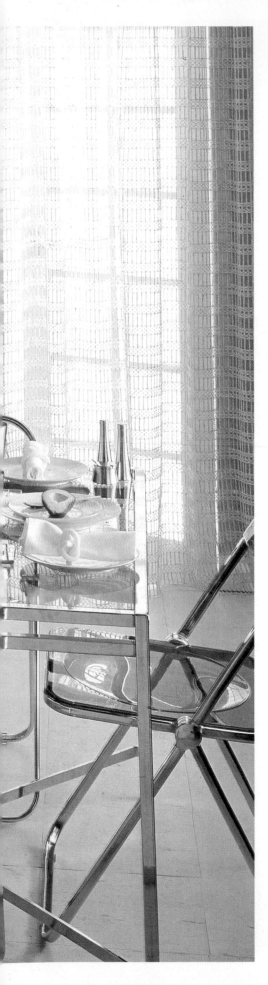

# Family Circle

# HOME ENTERTAINING

**Albany Books**

Designed and produced by
Albany Books
36 Park Street London W1Y 4DE

First published 1980

Published by Albany Books

Copyright © Albany Books 1980

Printed in Hong Kong

ISBN 0 86 136 071 0

*This text has previously been
published in issues of* Family Circle.
*The publishers wish to thank the
Editor and staff of the magazine for
their help in preparing it for this
edition. They also gratefully
acknowledge the loan of transparencies
from* Family Circle.

*Design : Tony Spaul*

The recipes contain both metric
and imperial measurements: these
are not always exact equivalents,
so do not mix them up.

# Contents

# Setting the Mood for Parties

A happy, relaxed atmosphere in which people can laugh and sparkle a little more brightly than usual is the aim of every host or hostess. But this kind of mood rarely just happens. It needs a bit of stage-setting to help it along. When setting the mood for any kind of party—whether it's two for dinner, or thirty for drinks—the very first essential is the lighting. One bright, glaring, central light is just about the biggest conversational handicap that any hosts can give their guests. The right, cosy kind of lighting can be achieved with wall, standard or table-lamps.

An easy way to make the most ordinary dining room look glamorous is to have lighted candles on the table. Candlelight makes everything look special, and looks lovely on a buffet table too.

These days it is easy to add the elegant touches that make everything look better, by contacting one of the many hire firms. In addition to hiring out every form of crockery, cutlery and glass, many of these firms have a very wide range of extras like ice-buckets, silver candelabra and punch bowls, and their charges are usually very reasonable.

At the dinner table, the way the food is presented can make the most economical meal look inviting. Little touches like making the butter into small rolls or serving a fresh fruit salad in a hollowed-out melon can make the difference.

*Left: Little touches such as candles, fresh flowers and cosy lighting help to create the ideal atmosphere for a successful dinner party. (Nairn Floors Information Service)*

*Right: It is always worth ensuring that the table is neatly and carefully laid, with everything attractively set out.*

Give a thought to the colour scheme in food as well as flowers and table-linen. Never serve two green vegetables, for instance—instead, contrast the green with the red of tomatoes or the orange of carrots.

In setting the table, try to allow at least 24 inches of table space for each guest. See that a man doesn't sit next to his wife, that the sexes are alternated as far as possible and that any unaccompanied person is placed next to you or your husband. Place the cutlery for each dinner starting at the outside for the first course and working towards the plate position for each following course. Dessert cutlery can be placed above. A bread plate is set to the left of each place, with a

neatly folded napkin on it. A bread roll may be laid on the napkin. Wine glasses are placed to the right of the cutlery, and in line with the tip of the large knife.

It is worth taking the extra minute to check that everything is laid in a geometrically precise position. Cutlery lying the slightest bit askew can give a surprisingly messy look to the table.

If your table has the beautiful gleam of burnished wood, you will want to show it to advantage. Use individual place mats and set each person's place on those. If the wood bears the marks of an over-zealous family, cover it with your prettiest tablecloth. Here, it's up to you to set whatever mood you choose. If your dinner plates are

heavily patterned, use a plain cloth; if you have a gay seersucker tablecloth, keep to the country style it conjures up with coloured earthenware and a jug of homely garden flowers. If you are dressing up your table with a snowy white cloth, you can afford to be more formal in your choice of flowers.

Flowers can play an immense part in enhancing a room or table. Remember the mood you are out to create when choosing the colours. At a winter party or dinner, the mood should be of welcoming warmth, a cosy glow, and here flowers of red, rose, vermilion, crimson or orange will help most. Green leaves have a 'cooling' effect, so keep them to a minimum in winter. Warm copper beech leaves, however, are ideal. On a warm summer's day,

flower arrangements in yellow or white, or green leaves, can look coolly refreshing.

Keep in mind the background, too. Blue and mauve flowers, for instance, look lovely when there is silver on the table, a bowl of white flowers superb on a dark polished table.

Of course, there are very many ways in which flowers can be arranged. For dining tables, remember the basic rule that the flower arrangement must always be low, then don't be afraid to use your imagination. Often the simplest ideas are the most effective— one white marguerite on each red napkin and a low bowl of the same flowers in the centre; simple garden nasturtiums, with trailing ones at each side to give a long, low arrangement, ideal for an oblong

dinner table; or a circlet of ivy in the centre with trailing ends.

Take practical considerations into account too. Make sure that room temperatures are comfortable, so that guests move from one pleasant atmosphere to another. See that the bathroom's clean and tidy, with fresh tablets of soap and hand towels. Clear away treasures that might get broken. Provide plenty of mats for glasses, and plenty of ashtrays—the bigger the better. Make sure bowls of flowers are well out of elbow-swinging range, and clear away unnecessary bits of furniture to leave plenty of floor room.

Below: *Here flowers, table cloth and crockery have been thoughtfully chosen to match the room's colour scheme.*

# Planning the Menu

Too much last-minute cooking makes a hostess harassed, so plan food that can be prepared in advance. With a hot main course, a cold dessert is practical and a cold or quickly heated first course.

Variety is the secret of an attractive meal—variety of types of food, flavour, colour and richness. Avoid serving the same food in more than one course. For example, if the main course is meat, serve fish or a vegetable starter and a fruit dessert. First decide the main course, then plan the vegetables and other courses to complement it.

The following list will give you an idea of how much food to allow per person, whether you're catering for a small dinner party, buffet party, or a large gathering.

Below: *A mouthwatering display of food for a buffet party.*

## Savouries and Snacks

**Sausage rolls:** Allow 2 per portion—20 rolls to 450g (1lb) pastry, 450g (1lb) sausage meat or sausages.

**Sausages on sticks:** Allow 2 per portion—16 chipolatas per 450g (1lb).

**Patties or vol-au-vents:** Allow 2 per portion.

**Cheese straws:** Allow 6 per portion—200g ($\frac{1}{2}$lb) cheese pastry makes 100.

**Stuffed eggs or tomatoes:** Allow 1 per portion.

**Sandwiches:** Allow 1 round per portion—1 thin cut loaf has approximately 20 slices; allow 100g to 150g (4oz to 6oz) butter for spreading and 650g (1$\frac{1}{2}$lb) cheese, 8 eggs or 300g (12oz) cooked meat for filling.

**Open sandwiches:** Allow 2 per portion.

**Cheese:** 450g (1lb) assorted cheeses serves 4 portions.

**French bread:** 30cm (12in) stick gives 6 slices.

**Butter:** 200g ($\frac{1}{2}$lb) serves 8 portions.

**Biscuits** — quantities per 450g (1lb): Plain—30 biscuits; cream filled—36 biscuits; cream crackers —50 biscuits.

## By the Plate

**Poultry:** 450g (1lb) sliced cold serves 6 to 8 portions.

**Ham:** 450g (1lb) sliced cold serves 6 to 8 portions.

**Savoury flans:** 20cm to 25cm (8in to 10in) flan cuts into 12 portions.

**Mixed salad:** 1 lettuce, 1 head celery, 200g ($\frac{1}{2}$lb) tomatoes, $\frac{1}{2}$ cucumber and 2 hard-boiled eggs serves 6 portions.

## For a Dinner Party

**Soup:** Allow 250ml ($\frac{1}{3}$ pint) per portion.

**Meat:** Allow 100g to 125g (4oz) fresh uncooked meat per portion.

**Fish:** Allow 50g (2oz) cooked shell fish per portion; 125g to 150g (5oz to 6oz) uncooked white fish per portion; 125g to 150g (5oz to 6oz) uncooked salmon per portion.

**Vegetables:** 450g (1lb) potatoes serves 3 to 4 portions; 450g (1lb) green vegetables serves 3 to 4 portions; 1 large cauliflower serves 5 to 6 portions; allow 2 tomatoes per portion.

**Rice or pasta:** Allow 50g (2oz) per portion.

**Gâteaux:** 20cm (8in) gateau serves 8 to 12 portions.

## Jellies / Trifle etc.

**Jellies:** One packet serves 6 portions.

**Trifle:** 1 litre (2 pints) dish serves 8 portions.

**Cream:** 125ml ($\frac{1}{4}$ pint) double cream serves 6 portions; 125ml ($\frac{1}{4}$ pint) single cream serves 8 portions, when served with fruit.

**Cakes:** 15cm (6in) layer or sandwich cake 5cm (2in) deep serves 6 portions; 20cm (8in) layer or sandwich cake 5cm (2in) deep serves 8 portions; 22cm (8$\frac{1}{2}$in) square tin 6cm (2$\frac{1}{2}$in) deep serves 16 portions. 15cm (6in) Madeira cake serves 8 portions; 450g (1lb) slab of cake serves 8 portions; 3kg (6lb) slab of cake serves 44 portions.

## Beverages

**Tea:** 75g (2$\frac{1}{2}$oz) makes 32 cups; allow 750ml (2 pints) milk and 450g (1lb) sugar.

**Coffee:** 50g (2oz to 3oz) makes 20 medium-sized cups; allow 1 litre (2 pints) milk and 450g (1lb) sugar; 50g (2oz) instant coffee makes 25 cups: allow 1·5 litres (1$\frac{1}{2}$ pints) milk and 600g (1$\frac{1}{4}$lb) sugar.

**Fruit squashes:** 1 litre bottle makes 25 glasses.

## Wines and Spirits

**Wine:** 1 bottle serves 6 glasses; 1 litre serves 9 glasses.

**Champagne and sparkling wine:** 1 bottle serves 6 to 8 glasses.

**Vermouths (Martini, Dubonnet):** 1 bottle straight serves 16 to 20 glasses.

**Sherry and port:** 1 bottle serves 12 to 16 glasses.

**Whisky, gin, brandy:** 1 bottle serves 20 to 24 measures.

**Liqueurs:** 1 bottle serves 20 to 24 measures.

Left: *Wine is the perfect drink for any party or special occasion.* (Spectrum Colour Library)

# Wine Sense

## Choosing Wines

Most people start by drinking wine with their meals, then move on to the equally enjoyable custom of serving wine on social occasions, as an alternative to spirits. Not only does this add a distinguished note to the proceedings, but it's economical, too, particularly when you're entertaining on a large scale.

With food, you should always try to match the wine to the dish you are serving. For example, a succulent joint of beef is perfectly partnered by a rich, red Burgundy, whereas a lighter Claret would be a better partner for lamb, and so on. White meats and seafoods harmonise perfectly with the light and dry qualities of a white Burgundy or Riesling. The guide line is no more complicated than this: full-flavoured wines for strong-flavoured foods, lighter wines for delicate ones.

## Glasses

It is not just a question of whether glasses look nice; their shape is functional, too. For example, a sadly high proportion of champagne is served in those saucer-like glasses that caterers are so fond of, but these glasses rapidly disperse the bubbles that are the very life of the champagne, together with all the wine's delightful bouquet. Champagne should be served in a tulip-shaped glass.

White wines should be served, chilled, in glasses with very long stems. This is not only because the glasses look elegant: by holding that long stem, you prevent your hand from warming the wine.

*Right: The tulip-shaped champagne glass (left) retains the bubbles, while in the saucer-shaped glass (centre) they rapidly disperse. On the right, a long-stemmed white wine glass. (Spectrum Colour Library)*

## Serving Wines

Always serve red wines at room tenperature, but never warm them up artificially by putting the bottles in warm water or standing them in front of the fire. Open the bottles an hour or so before serving, to allow the wine time to 'breathe'.

With white wines, you won't go wrong if you remember that the sweeter they are, the colder you should serve them. But don't make them too cold—no more than two hours in the refrigerator is necessary.

Once you start to know your way around the main wine types, you'll find that you get an extra pleasure from their bouquet. To make the most of this aroma, never fill the glasses more than two-thirds full.

## Wine for a Party

'A meal without wine is like a day without sun', says the old French proverb. There's no need to feel that you have to be an expert in order to enjoy a glass of wine with your dinner. Don't be put off by the length of the wine list or the variety of bottles bearing foreign labels.

For buffet parties, wine is a popular drink with both host and guests; it's simple to serve and economical, too. The normal-sized wine bottles hold about six glasses, the litre bottles eight to nine. Some wines are also available in gallon jars, which are ideal for large quantities of wine cups or punches, but difficult for pouring into individual glasses. If you buy wine like this, pour it into a jug for serving.

When ordering wine for parties it is usual to do so on a sale or return basis. Don't have too many types to choose from or the chances are you will be left with many half-finished ones, which are, of course, not returnable. A red, white and a rosé wine is a good selection. Some retailers will be happy to lend you the glasses you need, but do give them fair warning of your requirements. For Christmas and New Year parties, let them know at the beginning of December the numbers you require; at other times, two weeks' notice is usually sufficient. Order more glasses than the number of guests you expect, in case of breakages and to allow for people putting down glasses, and forgetting them, or for changing from one wine to another.

Wine cups and mulled wines are increasing in popularity; they're inexpensive and very enjoyable. There is no need for the host to spend the whole evening stirring his hot brew. You serve a mulled wine or a hot wine cup because it's cold outside, so either offer it to your guests as they arrive, or just before they leave.

14

# Party Drinks

## CELEBRATION CUP

1 bottle sparkling white wine
1 small (50g: 2oz) jar maraschino
    cherries
1 (250ml: 10fl.oz) bottle
    lemonade
1 lemon

1. Chill the wine.
2. Drain the maraschino cherries and place the syrup in a large jug with the wine and lemonade. Stir thoroughly.
3. Cut the lemon into 8 thin slices and spear a cherry in the centre of each slice with a cocktail stick.
4. Place a cherry and lemon slice in the bottom of 8 glasses (use champagne type if available) and pour over the wine. Serve at once. Makes 8 glasses.

## MULLED PORT

15ml (1 level tablespoon) moist
    brown sugar
8 cloves
$\frac{1}{2} \times 2 \cdot 5$ml spoon ($\frac{1}{4}$ level teaspoon)
    ground ginger
$\frac{1}{2} \times 2 \cdot 5$ml ($\frac{1}{4}$ level teaspoon)
    cinnamon
Rind and juice of 1 lemon
570ml (1 pint) water
Juice of 1 orange
1 bottle port-type wine

1. Place sugar, cloves, ginger, cinnamon and lemon rind in a saucepan. Add water and bring to boil. Cover, remove from heat and leave to infuse for $\frac{1}{2}$ hour. Then strain.
2. Add strained lemon and orange juice and wine. Heat, but do not boil.
3. Serve hot. Makes 10 to 15 glasses.

Left: *Home-made party drinks are colourful, unusual and appealing.* (Spectrum Colour Library)

## SANGRIA

250ml ($\frac{1}{2}$ pint) water
200g ($\frac{1}{2}$lb) sugar
1 small orange
1 small lemon
1 apple
Ice cubes
1 bottle red wine
$6 \times 15$ml spoons (6 tablespoons)
    brandy
A few slices cucumber
Soda water

1. Place water and sugar in a saucepan and bring to boil, stirring. Boil for 5 minutes.
2. Wash fruit and slice thinly, leaving peel and skin on. Remove core from apple. Place in a bowl, pour syrup over and leave for 2 hours.
3. Fill a large glass jug with a tray of ice cubes; add the fruit, 125ml ($\frac{1}{4}$ pint) of the syrup, red wine, brandy and cucumber slices. Stir with a wooden spoon, then add soda water to taste, about 150ml (6fl.oz). Makes about 12 glasses.

## TORTEVAL PUNCH

6 cloves
$\frac{1}{2} \times 2 \cdot 5$ml spoon ($\frac{1}{4}$ level teaspoon)
    cinnamon
$\frac{1}{2} \times 2 \cdot 5$ml spoon ($\frac{1}{4}$ level teaspoon)
    nutmeg
250ml ($\frac{1}{2}$ pint) water
Rind and juice of $\frac{1}{2}$ lemon
1 quarter-bottle whisky
$2 \times 15$ml spoons (2 tablespoons)
    lime juice cordial
$2 \times 5$ml spoon (1 rounded
    teaspoon) sugar
125ml ($\frac{1}{4}$ pint) ginger beer

1. Place cloves, cinnamon and nutmeg in a saucepan. Add water and thinly pared rind of lemon. Bring to boil, remove from heat and leave to infuse for $\frac{1}{2}$ to 1 hour.
2. Strain into a jug and rinse out saucepan. Return to saucepan and add strained lemon juice, whisky, lime juice cordial and sugar. Heat gently but do not boil.
3. Just before serving, add ginger beer and heat. Serve in small glasses. Makes 12 small glasses.

## BURGUNDY CUP

1 bottle red burgundy
1 miniature bottle orange liqueur
125ml ($\frac{1}{4}$ pint) ginger beer
125ml ($\frac{1}{4}$ pint) lemonade
Ice cubes

1. Mix burgundy and orange liqueur together in a large jug and leave in a cool place for $\frac{1}{2}$ to 1 hour.
2. Just before serving, add ginger beer and lemonade, and float ice cubes on top. Serve immediately. Makes 10 glasses.

## ANDALUSIAN CUP

1 orange
1 lemon
1 bottle medium sweet sherry
$3 \times 15$ml spoons (3 tablespoons)
    brandy
1 siphon soda
Ice cubes

1. Pare a few strips of rind from orange and lemon, using a sharp knife or a potato peeler. Cut into fine strips and place in a bowl.
2. Squeeze juice from orange and lemon and add, together with sherry and brandy. Leave in a cool place for 1 hour.
3. Just before serving, add soda water and ice cubes. Makes about 15 small glasses.

# Giving a Cheese and Wine Party

A cheese and wine party is simplicity itself to prepare and it's comparatively inexpensive too. The food can be elaborate or straightforward, and you can prepare for large numbers of guests quite easily.

For food, all you need is about six varieties of cheese; choose two each from the hard cheeses, such as Cheddar and Dutch; two blue cheeses, such as Stilton, Gorgonzola or Danish Blue; two creamy cheeses, like Camembert, Brie or cream cheese. Have baskets of wholemeal, rye and French breads, also a selection of cracker biscuits. You can fill some of the attractive loaves available these days with savoury cheese fillings. Hot savoury cheese flans are delicious for a winter party, and dips with carrot sticks, celery and small savoury biscuits are always popular.

For a large party, a selection of white, rosé and red wines would be suitable, but, for a small party, white and one other wine would be adequate. If your party is a large one, it is often more economical to buy wines in litre or magnum bottles. Serve white and rosé wines chilled, and red wines at room temperature. Remove the corks of red wine bottles about an hour before serving, to allow the wine to 'breathe'. Allow half a bottle of wine for each guest. You might also serve a welcoming hot wine cup, which is easy to serve and inexpensive.

Below: *The basic requirements – fresh cheese, bread, and a choice of wines.* (Spectrum Colour Library)

# Menu Matters

An evening spent with friends or relatives over a delicious meal is very pleasant. It is so easy, too—we have planned two complete menus for you to try when next you're entertaining, both designed to fit into the busy lives we all lead. Perhaps you're out all day and want to prepare the meal in advance, leaving it to cook in a time-controlled oven, or want to celebrate on a special occasion. Besides the recipes, we've worked out the order of preparing the dishes, to make it easy.

## For a special occasion
*Serves 6*

*Onion and Cheese Flan*

*Mixed Grill with Garlic Butter*

*Sauté Potatoes*

*Green Salad with French Dressing*

*Strawberry Foam Ring*

Wine to Serve with the main course:
*Beaujolais Villages* (red) or *Niersteiner* (white)

**Prepare meal in this order:**
*On the previous day*
1. Prepare and cook cake for Strawberry Foam Ring. Store in a cake tin.
2. Prepare Garlic Butter; leave in refrigerator. Make French Dressing.
3. Rub in pastry ingredients for Onion and Cheese Flan. Place in a polythene bag; keep in a cool place. If serving the flan cold, complete the dish and cook.

Above: *Onion and cheese flan.*

*During day of dinner party*
1. Make pastry, line flan ring, cover and keep in a cool place.
2. Prepare the potatoes; parboil and cover with foil.
3. Wash salad ingredients; place in a polythene bag.
4. Prepare lamb cutlets, kidneys, sausages and tomatoes. Cover with foil and keep in a cool place.
5. Fill cake and cover with strawberry mixture; leave in a cool place.
*One hour before serving*
1. Prepare a moderate oven (190 deg C, 375 deg F, Gas Mark 5).
2. Arrange salad in salad bowl.
3. Decorate Strawberry Foam Ring.
4. Complete Onion and Cheese Flan (if serving hot) and place in oven.
5. Prepare a moderate grill and grill lamb cutlets, sausages, kidneys and tomatoes; keep hot.
6. Meanwhile, slice and sauté the potatoes; keep hot.

## ONION AND CHEESE FLAN

*For 6 portions*

**Filling**
300g ($\frac{3}{4}$lb) onions
25g (1oz) margarine
1 standard egg
1 standard egg yolk
125ml ($\frac{1}{4}$ pint) milk
2×5ml spoons (2 level teaspoons) salt
$\frac{1}{2}$×2·5ml spoon ($\frac{1}{4}$ level teaspoon) pepper
50g (2oz) Cheddar cheese

**Shortcrust Pastry**
100g (4oz) plain flour
$\frac{1}{2}$×2·5ml spoon ($\frac{1}{4}$ level teaspoon) salt
25g (1oz) margarine
25g (1oz) lard
Cold water to mix
Sprig of parsley

1. Prepare a moderate oven (190 deg C, 375 deg F, Gas Mark 5). Place a plain 18cm (7in) flan ring on a baking sheet.

**2.** Peel and finely slice onions. Melt margarine in a frying pan; add onions and fry for about 6 minutes, until deep golden brown. Turn out on to a plate; leave to cool.

**3.** Beat egg, egg yolk and milk together in a basin. Add 2 × 5ml spoons (2 level teaspoons) salt and the pepper. Grate cheese. (Use egg white in Strawberry Foam Ring. See recipe on page 00.)

**4.** Place flour and salt in a bowl. Add fats, cut into small pieces, and rub in with the fingertips until mixture resembles fine bread-crumbs. Add about 1 × 15ml spoon (1 tablespoon) cold water and mix with a fork to form a firm dough.

**5.** Turn out on to a floured board and knead lightly. Roll out to a circle, 4cm (1½in) larger all around than flan ring. Support pastry on rolling pin and lift on to flan ring. Gently ease pastry into flan ring. Roll off surplus pastry with rolling pin across top of flan.

**6.** Sprinkle half of grated cheese on base of flan case. Place onions on top. Strain egg mixture into flan case; sprinkle with remaining cheese.

**7.** Bake in centre of oven for 30 to 35 minutes until filling is set and pastry is golden brown. Remove flan ring 10 minutes before end of cooking time. Garnish with a sprig of parsley. Serve warm or cold.

## MIXED GRILL
*For 6 portions*

6 best end neck of lamb cutlets
6 lambs' kidneys
6 back bacon rasher
6 sausages
6 small tomatoes
Salt and pepper
Sprigs of watercress or parsley

### Garlic Butter
50g (2oz) butter
1 × 2·5ml spoon (½ level teaspoon) garlic salt
1 × 5ml spoon (1 teaspoon) lemon juice

Left: *Mixed grill with sauté potatoes and green salad.*

1. Cream butter, garlic salt and lemon juice together in a small basin. Cut a piece of greaseproof paper 13cm by 7·5cm (5in by 3in); dampen greaseproof paper. Place butter mixture on the greaseproof paper; form into a roll 7·5cm (3in) long. Wrap in greaseproof paper; leave in a cool place until firm.
2. Trim cutlets. Remove any fat from kidneys; cut kidneys in halves and remove skin and cores. Cut bacon rashers in halves; wrap a piece of bacon around each kidney half. Twist each sausage in the centre; cut to make two small sausage. Score skin of each tomato in a cross.
3. Prepare a moderate grill.
4. Place cutlets and sausages on grill rack; sprinkle cutlets with a little salt and pepper. Grill for 8 to 10 minutes, turning cutlets and sausages once. Place on a warmed dish; keep hot.
5. Place tomatoes and kidneys on grill rack; sprinkle tomatoes with a little salt and pepper. Grill for 8 to 10 minutes, turning kidneys once. Place on a warmed dish; keep hot.
6. To serve: arrange cutlets down centre of a large, warmed oval serving dish. Place 3 tomatoes at each end of dish and kidneys and sausages down each side. Garnish with sprigs of watercress or parsley. Cut garlic butter into 6 slices; place a slice on each cutlet. Serve immediately with Green Salad and Sauté Potatoes (see recipes).

## SAUTE POTATOES
*For 6 portions*

1kg (2lb) potatoes
100g (4oz) butter or margarine
Salt

1. Wash potatoes; place in a saucepan of cold water. Bring to boil; cook for 5 to 10 minutes,
according to size of potatoes, to parboil.
2. Drain potatoes; leave to cool slightly, then peel and cut into 6mm (¼in) slices.
3. Heat butter or margarine in a large frying pan; add potatoes and some salt. Fry until golden brown, turning once.
4. Drain on kitchen paper; place in a warmed serving dish and serve with Mixed Grill and Green Salad (see recipes).

## GREEN SALAD WITH FRENCH DRESSING
*For 6 portions*

Lettuce
Cucumber
Watercress
Half a green pepper

### French Dressing
2 × 15ml spoons (2 tablespoons) oil
1 × 15ml spoon (1 tablespoon) vinegar
½ × 2·5ml spoon (¼ level teaspoon) salt
½ × 2·5ml spoon (¼ level teaspoon) sugar
Pinch of pepper

1. Wash lettuce and remove any coarse leaves; tear the larger leaves. Place lettuce in a salad bowl.
2. Cut cucumber into thin slices (remove skin, if preferred). Place in salad bowl.
3. Wash watercress; discard coarse stalks. Place in salad bowl.
4. Discard seeds, core and white pith from green pepper; cut pepper into strips. Add to salad bowl.
5. Make French Dressing. Place all ingredients in a small basin and beat with a fork. Alternatively, place in a small screw-topped jar or firmly-closed plastic container and shake vigorously. Sprinkle over salad just before serving.

*Note:* Wine vinegar or tarragon vinegar used in French dressing gives a better flavour than malt vinegar.

19

## STRAWBERRY FOAM RING
*For 6 portions*

### Cake
2 standard eggs
50g (2oz) castor sugar
50g (2oz) plain flour
1 × 2·5ml spoon (½ level teaspoon) baking powder

### Filling and topping
1 medium-sized orange
1 (200g: 8oz) pack frozen strawberries, just thawed
Castor sugar
1 standard egg white

1. Prepare a moderately hot oven (200 deg C, 400 deg F, Gas Mark 6). Brush a 1-litre (2-pint) fluted ring mould with oil or with melted fat.
2. Bring a saucepan of water to the boil; remove from heat. Place 2 eggs and 50g (2oz) castor sugar in a bowl over saucepan and whisk until mixture becomes thick and leaves a trail when whisk is lifted. Remove bowl from saucepan and continue whisking until mixture is cool.
3. Sift flour and baking powder together; carefully fold into egg mixture, cutting through the mixture with a metal spoon.
4. Pour mixture into prepared mould; shake mould gently to level mixture. Bake on shelf just below centre of oven for 25 minutes. Remove from mould; leave to cool on a wire rack.
5. Cut cake in half horizontally. Cut 3 thin slices from centre of orange, wrap in foil and reserve for decoration. Squeeze juice from remainder of orange. Reserve 2 × 5ml spoons (2 teaspoons) juice and spoon remainder over halves of cake
6. Reserve 6 strawberries for decoration; keep in refrigerator until required. Slice half of remaining strawberries; place in a basin and add 1 × 15ml spoon (1 level tablespoon) castor sugar. Sandwich cake together with strawberry and sugar mixture. Place cake on a serving plate.
7. Place remaining half of strawberries in a clean, grease-free mixing bowl; whisk until pulped. Add egg white, 3 × 15ml spoons (3 level tablespoons) castor sugar and reserved orange juice. (Use egg yolk in Onion and Cheese Flan: see recipe on page 00). Bring a large saucepan of water to the boil; remove from heat. Place bowl over saucepan and whisk mixture with a rotary whisk or electric mixer until mixture stands in soft peaks when whisk is lifted, about 10 minutes. Remove bowl from saucepan and continue whisking until mixture stands in stiff peaks.
8. Using a round-ended knife, spread strawberry mixture over sponge, covering cake completely. Keep in a cool place until required.
9. Just before serving, cut reserved orange slices in halves. Arrange halved slices and reserved strawberries alternately around top of gâteau.

Below: *Strawberry foam ring.*

## Meal from the store cupboard
*Serves 4*

*Cream of Celery Soup with crispy bacon croûtons*

---

*Indian Summer Supper Dish*

*Boiled Rice*

*Peas*

---

*Grecian Banana Split*

Drinks to serve with the main course:
*Lager* or *Chablis*

---

### Prepare meal in this order:
1. Cook croûtons and bacon for the soup.
2. Heat soup, boil rice and cook peas.
3. Prepare Indian Summer Supper Dish.
4. Assemble the ingredients for Grecian Banana Split.

## CREAM OF CELERY SOUP
*For 4 portions*

1 large can condensed cream of
 celery soup
Milk

**Croûtons**
3 slices white bread from a large
 loaf
2 rashers streaky bacon
50g (2oz) margarine

**1.** Place soup in a saucepan; add a can of milk and water mixed.
**2.** Trim crusts from bread; cut bread into 6mm ($\frac{1}{4}$in) dice. Remove rind and bone from bacon; cut bacon into small pieces. Fry bacon until crisp; remove from pan and drain on kitchen paper. Melt margarine in frying pan and fry bread until golden; drain on kitchen paper. Mix bacon and bread together.
**3.** Heat soup and serve with the croûtons.

## GRECIAN BANANA SPLIT
*For 4 portions*

4 bananas
1 brick vanilla ice cream
Clear honey
Canned cream (optional)
Browned, flaked almonds

**1.** Peel bananas; cut each in half lengthwise.
**2.** Cut ice cream into 4 slices; place each slice, upright, on an individual plate between 2 banana halves.
**3.** Spoon a little honey over each slice of ice cream. Top with a spoonful of cream, if used, and sprinkle with almonds. Serve immediately.

## INDIAN SUMMER SUPPER DISH
*For 4 portions*

1 small 150g (6$\frac{1}{4}$oz) can red
 peppers
1 large 500g (15$\frac{1}{4}$oz) can
 vegetable salad
2 level teaspoons curry powder
1 (500g: 1lb) can chopped ham
 with pork
25g (1oz) margarine
Sprigs of parsley

**1.** Prepare a moderate grill. Drain liquor from can of red peppers; dry peppers on kitchen paper, then cut into 6mm ($\frac{1}{4}$in) pieces.
**2.** Place contents of can of vegetable salad in a small saucepan; stir in curry powder and half the peppers. Heat gently.
**3.** Cut chopped ham with pork into 4 equal slices. Place meat slices on grill rack; dot with margarine. Grill until lightly browned; remove from grill. Turn slices, dot with remaining margarine, return to grill and cook until lightly browned.
**4.** Arrange meat slices, over-lapping, in centre of a warmed ovenproof serving dish. Place curried vegetable mixture at each end of dish. Garnish meat with remaining red pepper and parsley. Serve with rice, peas.

## Leave-it-to-cook menu
*Serves 4*

*Smoked Fish Cocktail*

*Rosy Baked Chicken*

*Peas*

*Jacket Potatoes*

*Apricot Almond Flan*

*Whipped Cream*

Wine to serve
with the main course:
*Anjou Rosé*
or a branded rosé wine

**Prepare meal in this order:**

*On the previous day*

1. Prepare fish mixture for Smoked Fish Cocktail. Cover and leave in refrigerator until ready to serve.

2. Prepare chicken and place in a roasting tin; coat with basting sauce, pineapple and syrup. Cover with foil and leave in refrigerator until ready to set oven.

3. Prepare Apricot Almond Flan. Cover with foil and leave in a cool place until ready to set oven.

*During day of dinner party*

1. Prepare potatoes. Remove foil from prepared chicken and place, with potatoes, on shelf just above centre of oven. Remove foil from Apricot Almond Flan and place on shelf in lowest position in oven. Set oven control to moderate (190 deg C, 375 deg F, Eas Mark 5) and set time control for 1 hour before meal is to be served.

*30 minutes before end of cooking time*

Wash lettuce for Smoked Fish Cocktail and complete cocktail. Whip cream for Apricot Almond Flan.

*10 minutes before end of cooking time*

1. Cook peas, as directed on pack.
2. Complete Rosy Baked Chicken and Jacket Potatoes.
3. Dredge Flan with icing sugar.

---

## SMOKED FISH COCKTAIL
*For 4 portions*

---

2 standard eggs
1 (200g: 7½oz) carton frozen buttered smoked haddock
3 small gherkins
10×10ml spoons (5 rounded dessertspoons) mayonnaise
2×5ml spoons (2 teaspoons) lemon juice
Salt and pepper
8 lettuce leaves
1 thin slice lemon, quartered
Small sprigs of parsley

1. Hard boil eggs for 10 minutes. Crack and leave to cool in cold water; shell and dry on kitchen paper. Cook smoked haddock in bag, as directed on carton; drain fish, reserving liquor. Remove skin, flake fish; leave to cool.

2. Slice gherkins; place in a basin with mayonnaise, lemon juice, some salt, a shake of pepper and 1×10ml spoon (1 dessertspoon) fish liquor. Chop hard-boiled eggs and add to mixture, with flaked fish; mix well. Cover and leave in a cool place.

3. To serve: shred lettuce; place a little in base of each of 4 small glasses. Spoon fish mixture on top. Garnish each fish cocktail with lemon and sprigs of parsley.

Below: *Smoked fish cocktail.*

## ROSY BAKED CHICKEN
*For 4 portions*

4 chicken joints
1 small 200g (7¾oz) can sliced
  pineapple

**Sauce**
50g (2oz) margarine
1 × 15ml spoon (1 level
  tablespoon) plain flour
2 × 15ml spoons (2 level
  tablespoons) tomato ketchup
2 × 5ml spoons (2 level teaspoons)
  dry mustard
1 × 2·5ml spoon (½ level teaspoon)
  salt
Pepper
1 × 5ml spoon (1 teaspoon)
  Worcestershire sauce
1 × 15ml spoon (1 tablespoon)
  vinegar

1 (200g: ½lb) pack frozen peas
1 × 10ml spoon (1 level
  dessertspoon) cornflour

1. Remove skin from chicken joints. Wipe joints with kitchen paper and place in a large roasting tin.
2. Drain pineapple, reserving syrup in a small basin. Chop pineapple.
3. Place margarine in a basin and beat until soft and creamy. Beat in remaining sauce ingredients and half of chopped pineapple.
4. Spread mixture evenly over chicken joints. Pour pineapple syrup over and sprinkle with remaining chopped pineapple; cover with foil. If possible, leave in the refrigerator until ready to set the oven.
5. Remove foil and place on shelf just above centre of oven. Set oven control to moderate (190 deg C, 375 deg F, Gas Mark 5) and bake for 1 hour. Ten minutes before end of cooking time, cook peas, as

*Above: Rosy baked chicken with jacket potatoes.*

directed on pack. Place chicken joints on a warmed serving dish and keep hot while making gravy. Blend cornflour with a little water and stir into juices left in roasting tin. Cook gently for 3 minutes; pour over chicken joints. Arrange cooked, drained peas on dish around chicken or serve separately. Serve with Jacket Potatoes (see recipe).

23

## JACKET POTATOES
*For 4 portions*

4 medium-sized potatoes
Butter or margarine

1. Wash and scrub potatoes; re-move any eyes. Prick potatoes all over with a fork.
2. Place on shelf just above centre of oven. Set oven control to moderate (190 deg C, 375 deg F, Gas Mark 5) and bake for 1 hour.
3. Cut a cross in top of each potato; press gently at base to open. Top each potato with a knob of butter or margarine. Place potatoes in a warmed serving dish or a napkin-lined basket. Serve with Rosy Baked Chicken (see recipe).

Below: *Apricot almond flan.*

Right. (ZEFA)

## APRICOT ALMOND FLAN
*For 4 portions*

**Shortcrust pastry**
150g (6oz) plain flour
$\frac{1}{2} \times 2 \cdot 5$ml spoon ($\frac{1}{4}$ level teaspoon) salt
75g (3oz) mixed cooking fats
Cold water to mix

**Filling**
50g (2oz) margarine
50g (2oz) castor sugar
1 standard egg
A few drops almond essence
50g (2oz) ground almonds
1 (420g: 15oz) can apricot halves
$1 \times 15$ml spoon (1 level tablespoon) icing sugar

1. Place a 20·5cm (8in) fluted flan ring on a baking sheet.
2. Place flour and salt in a bowl. Add fats, cut into small pieces, and rub in with the fingertips until mixture resembles fine bread-crumbs. Add about $1\frac{1}{2} \times 15$ml spoons ($1\frac{1}{2}$ tablespoons) cold water and mix with a fork to form a firm dough. Turn out on to a floured board and knead lightly.
3. Roll out pastry to a circle 4cm ($1\frac{1}{2}$in) larger all around than flan ring. Support pastry on rolling pin and lift on to flan ring. Press into flutes of ring with the fingers. Roll off surplus pastry with rolling pin across top of flan ring. Press pastry into flutes again.
4. Cream 50g (2oz) margarine and castor sugar together in a bowl until light and fluffy. Beat eggs; add gradually, beating well after each addition. Stir in almond essence and ground almonds.
5. Place mixture in prepared flan case; level top with back of spoon. Drain apricot halves and dry on kitchen paper; arrange on top of almond mixture. Cover with foil. If possible, leave in the refrigerator until ready to set the oven.
6. Remove foil and place flan on shelf in lowest position in oven. Set oven control to moderate (190 deg C, 375 deg F, Gas Mark 5) and bake for 1 hour.
7. Dredge flan with icing sugar and serve with whipped cream.

24

# Christmas for Beginners

As hostess at Christmas, you have to produce lunch on time, cooked to perfection, and still look relaxed. That's quite a tall order, especially if it's the first time you have attempted this all-important meal. The secret is to start organising it weeks in advance, which is much easier than it sounds. Let us do all the planning for you. Just follow our countdown—which includes a full menu, shopping plan and recipes—for a traditional and very successful Christmas feast.

# CHRISTMAS DINNER MENU

*Melon*

*Roast Turkey★*
*with*
*Chestnut Stuffing★*

*Bacon Rolls★*

*Sausages*

*Roast Potatoes*

*Brussels Sprouts*

*Vichy Carrots★*

*Bread Sauce★*

*Cranberry Sauce*

*Christmas Pudding*
*with*

*Brandy Butter★*

*Mince Pies*

★Recipes given

Make your traditional rich Christmas pudding at least one month before Christmas. Cover the pudding with greaseproof paper, then store in a cool dry place.

*The first week in December:* Buy all the non-perishables.

*The second week in December:* Order the turkey. There always

Above: *Food prepared and ready for use at Christmas.*

seems to be a last minute rush for poultry at Christmas, so an early order is wise. A 3·5kg (7lb) oven-ready turkey will serve 10 to 12 portions; a 5kg (10lb) oven-ready turkey, 15 to 20 portions; and a 7·5kg (15lb) oven-ready turkey, 25 to 30 portions. If you buy a fresh bird, allow 1kg to 1·5kg (2½lb to 3lb) extra for the weight of the neck, legs and innards.

*The third week in December:* Make a batch of mince pies.

*Four days before Christmas:* Write out a shopping list of all the accompaniments for Christmas dinner—everything from cream, milk and vegetables to bacon and sausages—see our chart.

*Three days before Christmas:* If you're having a frozen turkey and it is a large bird, it could take anything up to 36 hours at room temperature to thaw, so now is the time to place it on a rack with a tray underneath to catch the drips. Prepare bread for the bread sauce. Once you have made the breadcrumbs, store them in paper bags; they go mouldy in plastic bags.

*Christmas Eve:* Prepare the bacon rolls. Halve the sausages by squeezing and twisting them in the centre, then cutting. Wrap up the bacon rolls and chipolatas in self-clinging plastic wrap; store in the refrigerator.

Make the brandy butter. Cover and store in the refrigerator.

It is always best to get all the vegetables out of the way. The potatoes can be peeled, placed in a large bowl and covered with cold water. The remaining vegetables, including onions for bread sauce and stuffing, can be prepared, washed, drained and stored in polythene bags in the refrigerator.

Next, for the gravy, simmer the giblets in a large saucepan with 1 pint of water for an hour. Strain and quickly cool the stock. Finally, prepare the stuffing. After this preparation, there should still be plenty of time for finishing off the table decorations and so on.

*Christmas Day:* Plan to serve the

lunch at 1pm, so have the bird cooked by 12.30. If you're serving white wine as well as red, make sure the white wine is placed in the fridge to chill, and the cork is drawn from the red wine, which should be at room temperature. Set the table.

Next, prepare the bird. The Christmas pudding needs between three and four hours of steaming, so put this on at 9 am. If you have a pressure cooker this will cut down the time. Keep a kettle of hot water at hand to top up the water in the steamer from time to time.

Parboil potatoes for 10 minutes before putting them into hot fat in a roasting tin below the turkey, 1 hour before the end of the cooking time. If you have already prepared the ingredients for the bread sauce, it's easy to make now and it can be kept warm by covering the container with foil and placing it on the floor of the oven. The bacon rolls and chipolata sausages just have to be added to the potatoes 25 minutes before the end of cooking time.

Half an hour before the meal is to be served, everything should be running smoothly: the turkey cooked, and the potatoes a rich, golden brown. Plates and serving dishes can be put in the warming drawer of your cooker.

Next, put the vegetables on to cook, turn off the oven, then remove the turkey from the roasting bag, place it on a warmed serving plate and keep it hot. Put the mince pies in to warm.

Quickly cut up the melon and put it on the table. The potatoes are next out of the oven to be transferred to a warmed vegetable dish. The bacon rolls and chipolatas should be placed around the turkey and everything put back into the oven (with the door ajar) to keep warm, until you're ready to eat it. There remains only the gravy to make and the vegetables to strain and put into dishes. Now put these in the oven, too. By 1.05 pm you should all be sitting down to eat a marvellous lunch.

The first course finished, this is when the man of the house plays his part, doubling as wine waiter and turkey carver. Carving is easy if you hold the leg with a paper napkin and cut through the joint, pulling the leg downwards and outwards to break it at the joint then cut it into two, a thigh and a drumstick. If it is large, slice the leg. Next, cut through the wing joint, taking a slice of the breast; then remove the wishbone. Slice the breast parallel with the breastbone.

After the main course, invert the pudding on to a warmed serving dish and decorate it with a sprig of holly. Serve it with the brandy butter — which will taste even better than when you made it.

To help you follow a shopping plan, work out how many people you will be catering for, and fill in amounts beside items on the left.

## Shopping list for our Christmas dinner menu

| Butcher | Amount |
|---|---|
| 1 oven-ready turkey | |
| Streaky bacon | |
| Sausages | |
| **Greengrocer** | |
| Honeydew melon | |
| Potatoes | |
| Brussels sprouts | |
| Carrots | |
| Parsley and watercress | |
| Lemon | |
| Onions | |
| Apple | |
| **Grocer** | |
| Bread | |
| Angelica and glacé cherries | |
| Icing sugar | |
| Peppercorns | |
| Large raisins, stoned | |
| Currants | |
| Sultanas | |
| Shelled almonds | |
| Mixed peel | |
| Margarine | |
| Lard | |
| Mincemeat | |
| Soft brown sugar (dark) | |
| Eggs | |
| Cloves | |
| Chestnut purée | |
| Cranberry sauce | |
| **Off Licence** | |
| Sherry, rum or brandy | |
| Wine | |

## ROAST TURKEY

1 oven-ready turkey
Melted butter

1. Prepare a moderate oven (180 deg C, 350 deg F, Gas Mark 4).
2. Remove giblets; rinse inside of bird with cold water and dry on kitchen paper. Place giblets in a saucepan with 750ml (1½ pints) water. Bring to boil, cover and simmer for 1 hour; strain.
3. Calculate cooking time of turkey by adding weight of stuffing ingredients to drawn weight of bird, to find total weight. Allow 30 minutes per kg (15 minutes per lb) up to 4kg (8lb), 24 minutes per kg (12 minutes per lb) from 4kg to 6kg (8lb to 12lb) and 20 minutes per kg (10 minutes per lb) from 6kg to 8kg (12lb to 16lb).
4. Stuff neck of bird with chestnut stuffing. Truss turkey with fine string. Brush the turkey with melted butter.
5. Prepare roasting bag as directed on packet or box. Place the turkey in bag and place in roasting tin.
6. Place in centre of oven and cook for calculated time. Roast potatoes in a tin on shelf below turkey; place in oven 1 hour before end of cooking time.
7. About 25 minutes before end of cooking time, place bacon rolls and chipolata sausages in a roasting tin on floor of oven.
8. When cooked, remove potatoes from tin. Remove tin with turkey from oven and lift out turkey, in bag. Slit bag and allow fat to run into tin.
9. Place turkey on a warmed serving plate; remove trussing string. Place the turkey in the oven, with heat turned off and door ajar, while making gravy.
10. Pour off most of fat from roasting tin; stir in flour. Add 570ml (1 pint) giblet stock, 1 × 5ml spoon (1 level teaspoon) salt and a shake of pepper. Bring to boil, stirring, then simmer for 3 minutes. Taste and add more seasoning if necessary, then strain into warmed gravy boat.
11. Just before serving, arrange bacon rolls and chipolata sausages around turkey. Serve with bread sauce and cranberry sauce.

## CHESTNUT STUFFING

1 small onion
200g (8oz) streaky bacon or bacon pieces
1 (450g: 15¾oz) can chestnut purée (unsweetened) or chestnut purée made from 700g (1½lb) chestnuts
1 × 5ml spoon (1 level teaspoon) sugar
Salt and pepper

1. Peel and finely chop onion. Remove rind and bone from bacon; cut bacon into small dice.
2. Place all ingredients in a bowl; mix well together. Use to stuff neck end of turkey.

## VICHY CARROTS

450g (1lb) carrots
25g (1oz) butter
2 × 5ml spoons (1 rounded teaspoon) castor sugar
½ × 2·5ml spoon (¼ level teaspoon) salt
2 × 5ml spoons (2 level teaspoons) chopped parsley

1. Scrape carrots and cut into rings.
2. Place in saucepan with butter, sugar and salt; heat until butter has melted, stirring continuously. Cover and cook over a low heat, until tender, about 20 to 25 minutes.
3. Stir in chopped parsley and pour carrots, with the butter, into a warmed serving dish.

## BACON ROLLS

100g (4oz) streaky bacon

1. Remove rind and bone from bacon. Stretch bacon rashers with the back of a knife. Cut in halves, across length. Roll up and place in a small roasting tin. Place on floor of oven about 25 minutes before end of cooking time.

## BREAD SAUCE

1 small onion
2 cloves
6 peppercorns
250ml (½ pint) milk
50g (2oz) fresh white breadcrumbs
25g (1oz) butter
1 × 2·5ml spoon (½ level teaspoon) salt

1. Peel and slice onion. Place in a small saucepan with cloves, peppercorns and milk. Cover and leave to infuse over a very low heat for 20 to 30 minutes. Strain milk into an ovenproof bowl or gravy boat.
2. Stir in breadcrumbs, butter and salt; leave in a warm place until bread has swollen. Place in oven to re-heat just before serving.

*Left: Roast turkey with trimmings.*

# CHRISTMAS PUDDING
*For 10 to 12 portions*

200g (8oz) fresh white
  breadcrumbs
50g (2oz) plain flour
200g (8oz) shredded suet
200g (8oz) soft brown sugar
  (dark)
200g (8oz) large raisins, stoned
200g (8oz) sultanas
200g (8oz) currants
50g (2oz) mixed peel
50g (2oz) shelled almonds
2×5ml spoons (1 rounded
  teaspoon) mixed spice
1 lemon
1 apple or carrot
4 standard eggs
3×15ml spoons (3 tablespoons)
  sherry, rum or brandy
Sprig of holly

1. Prepare a saucepan or steamer for cooking. Grease a 1-litre (2-pint) basin and a 250ml (½-pint) basin (or a 750ml/1½-pint basin and a 500ml/1-pint basin). Fit a circle of greaseproof paper in bottom of each basin; grease paper. Grease a double thickness of greaseproof paper for covering the puddings.
2. Place breadcrumbs in a large bowl; add flour, suet, sugar and dried fruit (if bought unwashed, wash on previous day and spread out to dry on baking sheets). Chop mixed peel and add to bowl.
3. Place almonds in a small saucepan, cover with water and bring to boil; strain off water and slip off skins. Shred almonds finely with a knife and add, with mixed spice, to bowl. Scrub lemon and grate rind into bowl; squeeze juice and add. Peel and grate apple or carrot and add. Beat eggs and add to bowl, together with sherry, rum or brandy. Mix all ingredients together thoroughly.
4. Fill basins with mixture and level tops with back of spoon. Make a pleat in greaseproof paper, to allow puddings to rise. Cover

*Left: Christmas pudding with brandy butter, and mince pies.*

basins and tie securely with string, making a loop over top of each basin, to form a handle. Steam each pudding for 6 hours, keeping pan of water filled with boiling water. (Alternatively, cook in a pressure cooker. Place 1 litre (2 pints) water in cooker and bring to boil. Place pudding on rack and close lid; steam for 1 hour. Place pressure weights on cooker and bring up to 15lb pressure; cook for 1 hour.) Replace paper covers with clean sheets of greaseproof paper. Tie down securely as before.
5. On Christmas Day, steam pudding for a further 3 to 4 hours (or 30 minutes in pressure cooker, followed by 30 minutes at 15lb pressure).
6. Invert pudding on to a warmed serving dish, remove circle of greaseproof paper and decorate top of pudding with a sprig of holly. Serve with brandy butter or custard.

*Note :* Silver charms may be inserted in pudding just before serving. Scrub and boil them before use.

Above: (ZEFA)

## BRANDY BUTTER

100g (4oz) butter
100g (4oz) castor sugar
4×15ml spoons (4 tablespoons)
  brandy (or to taste)
50g (2oz) glacé cherries
Angelica

1. Cream butter and sugar together until light and fluffy.

2. Beat in brandy a little at a time.
**To serve:** Chop glacé cherries and angelica; mix in, pile on to a serving plate. Leave in refrigerator to harden.

*Note :* Brandy Butter will keep for up to a week if stored in the refrigerator. Cover with foil.

## MINCE PIES
*Makes 12*

200g (8oz) plain flour
1×2·5ml spoon (½ level teaspoon)
  salt
50g (2oz) margarine
50g (2oz) lard
2×5ml spoons (2 level teaspoons)
  castor sugar
Cold water to mix

**Filling**
300g (¾lb) mincemeat
Icing sugar

1. Prepare a moderately hot oven (200 deg C, 400 deg F, Gas Mark 6).
2. Place flour and salt in a bowl. Add fats, cut into small pieces, and rub in with the fingertips until the mixture resembles fine breadcrumbs. Dissolve castor sugar in 1 × 15ml spoon (1 tablespoon) cold water and add. Add about 1 scant 15ml spoon (1 tablespoon) more water; mix to a firm dough.
3. Turn out pastry on to a floured board and knead lightly. Roll out pastry to 3mm (⅛in) thickness. Cut out 12 rounds, using a 8·5cm (3¼in) fluted cutter and press into each of 12 deep tartlet tins. Knead trimmings together; re-roll and cut out 12 more rounds, using a 5·5cm (2¼in) fluted cutter, for lids. Place heaped teaspoonsful of mincemeat in each pastry case. Dampen edges of lids; press into position and seal well. Snip top of each pie twice with scissors.
4. Place pies in centre of oven and bake for 20 to 25 minutes. Remove from tins, cool on a wire rack. Reheat before serving, if desired. Dredge tops of pies with icing sugar before serving.

# A Wedding Buffet Planned at Home

Whether you hire the church hall or have a buffet at home, our wedding buffet food will take the worry out of the catering.

It is essential to be able to prepare as much as possible in the weeks before the day, to save a panic at the last minute. A home freezer helps, but our food is all designed for keeping either in tins or in a refrigerator. When catering for large numbers, it's worth while to borrow a mixer or liquidiser, if you don't own one. Recruit some friends to help with the last-minute jobs, while you are at the ceremony.

Set the tables attractively and provide large, coloured paper napkins, perhaps the same colour as the flowers or the bridesmaids' dresses.

Crockery, cutlery and tables can often be hired.

It is customary to serve sherry to the guests after they've been greeted by the bride and groom and their parents at the reception. A dry white wine would be ideal to serve with the food.

For the toast to the bride and groom, it is traditional, though not essential, to have a sparkling wine. Choose a good-quality, non-vintage champagne or one of the other sparkling wines—Sparkling Vouvray, Sparkling White Burgundy, Gancia Spumante, Sparkling Hock and Spanish sparkling wine.

Below: *St. Clement's cheesecake.*

## ST. CLEMENT'S CHEESECAKE
*For 16 portions*

### Base
200g (3oz) digestive or Nice biscuits
2×15ml spoons (2 level tablespoons) golden syrup
2×15ml spoons (2 level tablespoons) cocoa
50g (2oz) butter

### Filling
25g ($\frac{3}{4}$oz) or 1$\frac{1}{2}$ envelopes gelatine
2 small oranges
1 small lemon
100g (4oz) castor sugar
450g (1lb) cottage cheese
1 (125ml: 6 fluid oz) carton double cream
2×15ml spoons (2 tablespoons) milk

### Decoration
4 orange slices
1 (50g: 2oz) bar plain chocolate

1. To make base: place biscuits between 2 sheets of greaseproof paper; crush finely with a rolling pin.
2. Measure golden syrup carefully, levelling off spoon with a knife and making sure there is none on underside of spoon. Place in a medium-sized saucepan, with cocoa and butter. Heat gently, stirring occasionally, until butter has melted; remove pan from heat and stir in biscuit crumbs.
3. Spread biscuit mixture in base of a round 21·5cm (8$\frac{1}{2}$in) loose-based cake tin; level top and press down lightly.
4. Make filling: measure 3×15ml spoons (3 tablespoons) cold water into a small basin and add gelatine. Place basin in a pan of water over a

moderate heat and stir until gelatine has dissolved. Remove basin from heat.

**5.** Scrub oranges and lemon; grate rind from fruits and place in a bowl. Squeeze juice from fruits; pour into a measuring jug.

**6.** Stir gelatine into juices and make up to 250ml ($\frac{1}{2}$ pint) with cold water. Add sugar and stir until dissolved.

**7.** Place cottage cheese in a sieve over bowl containing grated rind. Rub cheese through sieve with a wooden spoon.

**8.** Add fruit syrup mixture to bowl; mix well.

**9.** Place cream and milk in a basin, whisk until cream is just thick. Stir into cheese mixture in bowl.

**10.** Pour over biscuit base in tin; leave in a cool place to set.

**11.** Cut each orange slice in half; cut each half into 3 triangles.

**12.** Place flat side of chocolate on to working surface. Holding a long, sharp knife between the hands, at the point and handle, shave off thin layers of chocolate, at an angle, to form about 20 curls; keep in a cool place.

**13.** To remove cheesecake from tin: place tin on top of a 450g (1lb) size can; gently pull cake tin down from cheesecake. Ease cheesecake off base on to a plate with a palette knife.

**14.** Arrange a pile of chocolate curls in centre of cheesecake and orange triangles around top edge. Cut into 16 slices and keep in a cool place until ready to serve, or for up to 3 days in a refrigerator.

---

## STRAWBERRY MERINGUE BASKETS
*Makes 12*

---

4 standard egg whites
225g (9oz) icing sugar

**Filling**
450g (1lb) strawberries
2×15ml (2 tablespoons) Kirsch
2×15ml spoons (1 rounded tablespoon) castor sugar
1 (150ml: 6$\frac{2}{3}$ fluid oz) carton double cream
1 (125ml: 5 fluid oz) carton single cream

**1.** Heat oven at lowest setting; place shelves in coolest part.

**2.** Line 2 baking sheets with greaseproof paper. Draw 6 7·5cm (3in) circles, each a little apart, on each piece of greaseproof paper. Turn paper over and lightly brush circles with oil.

**3.** Half fill a saucepan with water; bring to boil, and remove from heat.

**4.** Place egg whites in a clean, grease-free bowl. Sieve icing sugar into bowl. Place bowl over saucepan of hot water and whisk until mixture becomes thick and leaves a trail when whisk is lifted.

**5.** Remove bowl from pan; continue whisking until mixture is cool.

**6.** Using a large piping bag, fitted with a No. 8 star tube, half fill with meringue mixture.

**7.** Pipe a ring of meringue inside marked line of one circle. Continue piping inside ring, to fill in centre with meringue. Pipe 2 more rings of meringue on to first ring, to form 'wall' of basket.

**8.** Make another 11 baskets and place in coolest part of oven for 2$\frac{1}{2}$ to 3 hours. Meringues should lift off paper easily. When meringues are cold, store in cardboard boxes for up to 4 weeks.

**9.** Make filling up to 5 hours before serving. Wash and hull strawberries. Reserve 12 for decoration; quarter remainder and place in a basin, with Kirsch and castor sugar. Mix together; cover and leave for at least 1 hour.

**10.** Strain syrup from strawberries and place in a bowl with chilled double and single creams. Whisk until cream holds its shape.

**11.** Add strawberries to cream mixture; fold in carefully with a metal spoon.

**12.** Divide mixture evenly between the meringue baskets; top each with a whole reserved strawberry. Store in a cool place.

better during cooking.

**10.** Prepare a moderately hot oven (200 deg C, 400 deg F, Gas Mark 6).

**11.** To bake blind: line each pastry case with a piece of greaseproof paper, 5cm (2in) larger than flan ring or tin.

**12.** Half fill with baking beans or rice and bake just above centre of oven for 15 minutes, to set pastry. Remove case from oven, lift out paper and baking beans or rice. Return to oven for a further 5 minutes, until pastry is cooked and pale golden in colour.

**13.** Remove flan ring and leave pastry flan case to cool on a wire rack; leave oblong pastry case in tin to cool.

*Note :* Pastry cases can be made and cooked up to one week in advance. Wrap pastry in self-clinging plastic film or foil and keep in a cool place.

## COTTAGE CHEESE AND SPINACH FLAN

*Makes 16 slices or squares*

1 cooked 25·5cm (10in) pastry flan case or a 34·5cm by 24cm (13½in by 9½in) pastry case

**Filling**

1 (150g: 6oz) carton frozen chopped spinach, just thawed

4 standard eggs

1 (125ml: 5 fluid oz) carton single cream

½ × 2·5ml spoon (¼ level teaspoon) ground nutmeg

½ × 2·5ml spoon (¼ level teaspoon) salt

2 × 15ml spoons (2 level tablespoons) Parmesan cheese

Pepper

1 (200g: 8oz) carton cottage cheese

**1.** Prepare a moderate oven (180 deg C, 350 deg F, Gas Mark 4).

**2.** Place pastry case on a baking sheet.

**3.** Place spinach in a sieve; press with a wooden spoon to remove excess water.

**4.** Place eggs, cream, nutmeg, salt, Parmesan cheese and a shake

*Above: In the foreground, right, is Seafood pâté. From there, reading clockwise, are Green salad, Egg, bacon and cheese flan, Corn and potato salad, Cottage cheese and spinach flan, and Kipper pâté.*

## PASTRY CASES

250g (10oz) plain flour

1 × 2·5ml spoon (½ level teaspoon) salt

125g (5oz) pastry margarine

Cold water to mix

**1.** Place a 25·5cm (10in) flan ring on a baking sheet, or use a 34·5cm by 24cm (13½in by 9½in) Swiss roll tin.

**2.** Place flour and salt in a bowl. Add margarine, cut into small pieces and rub in with the fingertips until mixture resembles fine breadcrumbs.

**3.** Add about 3½ × 15ml spoons (3½ tablespoons) cold water and

mix with a fork to form a firm dough.

**4.** Turn out on to a floured board and knead lightly.

**5.** To line a flan ring: roll out pastry to a circle 2·5cm (1in) larger all around than flan ring. Roll pastry around rolling pin and lift on to flan ring.

**6.** Gently ease pastry into flan ring and press into base and side of ring. Roll of surplus pastry with rolling pin across top of flan ring. Press pastry up the side again with the fingers. Prick all over with a fork.

**7.** To line an oblong tin: roll out pastry to an oblong, about 2·5cm (1in) larger all around than tin. Roll pastry around rolling pin and lift on to tin.

**8.** Gently ease pastry into tin and press into corners and up sides of tin. Cut off surplus pastry with a sharp knife across top of tin. Prick all over with a fork.

**9.** Place pastry cases in refrigerator for 30 minutes before cooking, as pastry will then keep its shape

of pepper in a bowl; beat together. Stir in cottage cheese and spinach.

5. Pour mixture into pastry case; bake in centre of oven for 30 to 35 minutes until mixture has set and feels firm.

6. When flan is cold, cut into 16 slices or squares.

*Note:* Flan can be made and cooked the day before it is required. Wrap flan in foil and keep in a cool place.

## EGG, BACON AND CHEESE FLAN
*Makes 16 slices or squares*

1 cooked 25·5cm (10in) pastry flan case, or a 34·5cm by 24cm (13½ by 9½in) pastry case

### Filling
6 rashers streaky bacon
150g (6oz) Cheddar cheese
4 standard eggs
1 (125ml: 6 fluid oz) carton single cream
125ml (¼ pint) milk
1 × 2·5ml spoon (¼ level teaspoon) salt
Pepper

1. Prepare a moderate oven (180 deg C, 350 deg F, Gas Mark 4).
2. Place pastry case on a baking sheet.
3. Remove rind and bone from bacon.
4. Prepare a moderate grill; place rashers on rack in grill pan and grill until crisp and golden brown.
5. Chop bacon finely; grate cheese. Sprinkle both over base of pastry case.
6. Place eggs, cream, milk, salt and a shake of pepper in a basin; beat together. Pour mixture into pastry case and bake in centre of oven for 30 to 35 minutes, until mixture has set and feels firm.
7. When flan is cold, cut into 16 slices or squares.

*Note:* Flan can be made and cooked the day before it is required. Wrap flan in foil and keep in a cool place.

## VEGETABLE FLAN
*Makes 16 slices or squares*

1 cooked 25·5cm (10in) pastry flan case or a 34·5cm by 24cm (13½in by 9½in) pastry case

### Filling
3 medium-sized tomatoes
2 medium-sized potatoes
1 medium-sized onion
Half a green pepper
50g (2oz) butter
4 standard eggs
1 × 2·5ml spoon (¼ level teaspoon) dried mixed herbs
1 × 2·5ml spoon (¼ level teaspoon) salt
Pepper

1. Prepare a moderate oven (180 deg C, 350 deg F, Gas Mark 4).
2. Place pastry case on a baking sheet.
3. Place tomatoes in a bowl and cover with boiling water. Leave for 1 minute; drain, then peel and chop finely.
4. Peel potatoes; cut into small dice. Peel and finely chop onion. Finely chop pepper.
5. Melt butter in a medium-sized saucepan. Add potatoes, onion and pepper and fry gently for 4 to 5 minutes. Remove saucepan from heat.
6. Place eggs, herbs, salt and a shake of pepper in a bowl; beat together. Stir in tomatoes and vegetables; pour into flan case.
7. Bake in centre of oven for 30 to 35 minutes, until egg has set and vegetables are tender.
8. When flan is cold, cut into 16 slices or squares.

*Note:* Flan can be made and cooked the day before it is required. Wrap flan in foil and keep in a cool place.

## SEAFOOD PATE
*For 14 to 16 slices*

25g (1oz) smoked salmon
1 (425g: 15oz) can mackerel in oil
1 (200g: 8oz) can mackerel in oil
150g (6oz) butter
2 × 15ml spoons (2 tablespoons) sherry
100g (4oz) fresh white breadcrumbs
Salt and pepper

### Garnish
Cucumber slices
Prawns

1. Line base and long sides of a 450g (1lb) loaf tin with foil, overlapping rim by 5cm (2in) at each side.
2. Trim smoked salmon to fit base of tin; arrange in tin.
3. Drain cans of mackerel; remove bones from fish.
4. Melt butter in a small saucepan; remove from heat.
5. Place one-third mackerel and one-third butter in liquidiser goblet. Run machine until contents are well blended. Pour mackerel mixture into a bowl. Repeat, using remaining mackerel and butter, blending half at a time.
6. Add sherry, breadcrumbs, a little salt and a shake of pepper to mackerel mixture; mix well.
7. Place mixture in tin, press down and level top with the back of a metal spoon.
8. Bring foil from each side of tin across top of tin to cover pâté. Place in refrigerator overnight or for up to 4 days.
9. Loosen pâté along short sides of tin with a palette knife, open foil across top of pâté and turn out on to a serving dish. Peel off foil carefully and slice pâté into 14 to 16 slices. Arrange on a serving dish and garnish with cucumber slices and prawns.

## KIPPER PATE
*For 14 to 16 slices*

2 × 250g (10oz) packs frozen
buttered kipper fillets, just
thawed
150g (6oz) butter
2 × 15ml spoons (2 tablespoons)
lemon juice
100g (4oz) fresh white
breadcrumbs
Pepper

**Garnish**
Mustard and cress or parsley
Lemon triangles

1. Line base and long sides of a
450g (1lb) loaf tin with foil, overlapping rim by 5cm (2in) at each
side.
2. Bring a large saucepan of water
to boil; add kippers and cook, as
directed on pack. Remove packs
from saucepan and leave to cool.
3. Melt butter in a small saucepan;
remove from heat.
4. Snip top of one pack of kippers
and empty contents into liquidiser
goblet; add half the melted butter
and run machine until contents
are well blended.
5. Place kipper mixture into a
bowl; repeat with remaining pack
of kippers, melted butter and
lemon juice. Stir breadcrumbs and
a shake of pepper into kipper
mixture and mix until well
blended.
6. Place mixture in tin, press
down and level top with the back
of a metal spoon. Bring foil from
each side of tin across top of pâté, to
cover top. Place in refrigerator
overnight or for up to one week.
7. Loosen pâté along short sides
of tin with a palette knife; open
foil across top of pâté and turn out
on to a serving dish. Peel off foil
carefully and slice pâté into 14 to
16 slices. Arrange on a serving
dish and garnish with mustard and
cress and lemon triangles.

*Right: In the foreground, left, is Vegetable
flan. From there, reading clockwise, are
Liver pâté, Tomato and onion salad,
Green rice salad, Carrot and orange salad,
and Celery, apple and nut salad.*

## LIVER PATE
*For 14 to 16 slices*

6 long rashers streaky bacon
200g (½lb) pigs' liver
25g (1oz) butter
1 medium-sized onion
1 clove of garlic
Salt
100g (4oz) sausagemeat
100g (4oz) fresh white
breadcrumbs
1 standard egg
1 × 5ml spoon (1 teaspoon)
anchovy essence
2 × 15ml spoons (2 tablespoons)
sherry
1 × 2·5ml spoons (½ level teaspoon)
mixed dried herbs
Pepper

1. Prepare a cool oven (170 deg
C, 325 deg F, Gas Mark 3). Half
fill a roasting tin with cold water.
2. Remove rind and bone from
bacon and press rashers flat with a
knife. Line the base and sides of a
450g (1lb) loaf tin with rashers;
press in firmly.
3. Remove any gristle from liver,
cut liver into small pieces.
4. Melt butter in a frying pan;
gently fry liver for 5 minutes.
Remove pan from heat.

*Above: A loving toast. (Colour Library
International)*

5. Peel onion, cut into small
pieces. Peel clove of garlic and place
on a saucer with a little salt. Using a
round-ended knife, rub salt against
garlic to crush clove.
6. Place garlic, sausagemeat,
breadcrumbs, egg, anchovy essence, sherry, herbs and a shake
of pepper in a bowl. Beat together
with a wooden spoon until well
mixed.
7. Place contents of frying pan
and the onion into liquidiser
goblet and run machine until
mixture is well blended.
8. Add liver mixture to bowl; mix
well.
9. Place liver mixture in tin; level
top with the back of a metal spoon.
Cover top of tin with a piece of foil
and place loaf tin in roasting tin.
10. Cook pâté in centre of oven
for 2 hours. Remove from oven,
take loaf tin out of water, loosen
foil, to allow steam to escape, and
leave pâté to become cold.
11. Turn pâté carefully out of tin,
wrap in extra foil and keep in
refrigerator for up to one week.
Cut into 14 to 16 slices. Arrange
on a serving dish and garnish with
lettuce.

## CELERY, APPLE AND NUT SALAD
*For 12 portion*

2×15ml spoons (2 tablespoons) lemon juice
2×15ml spoons (2 tablespoons) oil
6 sticks of celery
3 medium-sized dessert apples
Half a red pepper
50g (2oz) walnuts

1. Place lemon juice and oil in a bowl; whisk until thick.
2. Wash celery; chop finely and add to bowl.
3. Wash apples; cut each apple into quarters, remove cores and chop apples finely. Stir into celery and lemon dressing.
4. Chop pepper and walnuts finely, stir into celery and apple mixture.
5. Cover and leave in a cool place until required or overnight.

## GREEN RICE SALAD
*For 12 portions*

250g (10oz) long-grain rice
10cm (4in) piece of cucumber
Half a green pepper
20 stuffed olives
45ml (3 tablespoons) oil
15ml (1 tablespoon) wine vinegar
½ × 2·5ml spoon (¼ level teaspoon) dry mustard
Salt and pepper

1. Cook rice in a large saucepan of boiling, salted water for about 12 minutes. Test by pressing a grain between thumb and finger. Drain and rinse with cold water. Place in a large bowl.

2. Cut cucumber into small dice; chop pepper finely and slice olives. Mix cucumber, green pepper and olives into rice.

3. Place oil, vinegar, mustard, a little salt and a shake of pepper in a basin; whisk until thick.

4. Pour dressing into rice salad and mix lightly. Cover and leave in a cool place until required or overnight.

## TOMATO AND ONION SALAD
*For 12 portions*

8 medium-sized tomatoes
1 small onion
3×15ml spoons (3 tablespoons) oil
1×15ml spoon (1 tablespoon) wine vinegar
Salt and pepper

1. Wash tomatoes; slice thinly. Peel and thinly slice onion; separate each slice into rings.

2. Arrange slices of tomato and onion alternately, overlapping, in serving dishes. Cover and leave in a cool place until required.

3. Place oil, vinegar, a little salt and a shake of pepper in a basin. Whisk until thick, pour over tomatoes and onions just before serving.

## CARROT AND ORANGE SALAD
*For 12 portions*

700g (1½lb) carrots
3 small oranges
100g (4oz) seedless raisins
125ml (¼ pint) Mayonnaise (see recipe)

1. Peel carrots; grate finely and place in a large bowl.

2. Using a sharp or serrated knife, cut rind and pith from oranges, holding each orange over the bowl to catch the juice. Cut each orange into thin slices and each slice into 6 segments.

3. Add orange segments, raisins and mayonnaise to carrots and mix well.

4. Cover and leave in a cool place until required or overnight.

## CORN AND POTATO SALAD
*For 12 portions*

6 rashers streaky bacon
2 (540g: 1lb 3oz) cans potatoes
1 (175g: 7oz) can sweet corn
125ml (¼ pint) Mayonnaise (see recipe)

1. Remove rind and bone from bacon.

2. Prepare a moderate grill; place rashers on rack in grill pan and grill until crisp and golden brown.

3. Chop bacon finely; place in a large bowl.

4. Drain potatoes; cut into 6mm (¼in) dice and place in bowl.

5. Drain sweet corn thoroughly; stir into bowl with the mayonnaise and mix well.

6. Cover and leave in a cool place until required or overnight.

## MAYONNAISE

2 egg yolks
2×15ml spoons (2 tablespoons) wine vinegar
½×2·5ml spoon (¼ level teaspoon) salt
½×2·5ml spoon (¼ level teaspoon) dry mustard
Pinch of pepper
½×2·5ml spoon (¼ level teaspoon) sugar
250ml (½ pint) corn oil
1×15ml spoon (1 tablespoon) boiling water

1. Place egg yolks, vinegar, salt, mustard, pepper and sugar into liquidiser goblet and run machine until mixed. Remove small cap in lid, pour oil slowly into liquidiser in a steady stream on to rotating blades. Add boiling water and run machine until blended.

2. Store mayonnaise in air-tight container in a cold place for up to 3 weeks.

*Note:* Egg whites can be used for Strawberry Meringue Baskets (see recipe on page 33).

# Children's Parties

One of the greatest events in a child's life is his birthday. For most children, a party is the most popular celebration. Though children are usually too excited to eat, it is best to provide small, interesting items of food. Savoury foods are generally top favourites, and the most digestible.

Children love their own things, so try packing the food in individual cake boxes. This is a good idea if space is limited, as the table can be moved out to make room for games; the children can sit around a paper tablecloth on the floor, picnic fashion.

No birthday is complete without *the* cake, and we've designed some novel ones for you to try.

## MAGIC TOADSTOOLS
*Makes 12*

12 standard eggs
6 firm tomatoes
Mayonnaise or cream cheese

1. Hard boil eggs for 10 minutes; crack and leave in cold water to cool. Shell and dry on kitchen paper.
2. Trim base of each egg and stand pointed end upwards. Trim a little from the top of each egg.
3. Wash and cut tomatoes in halves. Fix one tomato half on top of each egg with a little mayonnaise or cream cheese.
4. Place some mayonnaise or cream cheese in a small greaseproof paper piping bag. Snip off end and pipe dots on tomatoes.

## CHEESE AND WATERCRESS TRIANGLES
*Makes 16*

75g (3oz) Cheddar cheese
200g (8oz) self-raising flour
Pinch of salt
1 × 2.5ml spoon (½ level teaspoon) dry mustard
50g (2oz) margarine
125ml (¼ pint) milk

**Watercress butter**
Half a bunch of watercress
100g (4oz) softened butter
Salt and pepper

Above: *Three years old today!* (Spectrum Colour Library)

1. Prepare a hot oven (220 deg C, 425 deg F, Gas Mark 7). Lightly grease a baking sheet. Grate cheese.
2. Sift flour, salt and mustard into a bowl. Add margarine, cut into small pieces and rub in with the fingertips until mixture resembles fine breadcrumbs.
3. Stir in cheese; add milk and mix lightly, to form a soft dough.
4. Turn out on to a floured board. Divide dough in half; roll each piece into a round, about 13cm (5in) in diameter. Cut across, to make 8 triangles. Place triangles on a baking sheet; brush tops with milk.
5. Bake just above centre of oven for 12 to 15 minutes, until golden brown. Leave to cool on baking sheet for a few minutes; remove from baking sheet and leave to cool completely on a wire rack.
6. Wash watercress; remove stalks and chop leaves coarsely. Place, with softened butter, in a bowl; mix together. Season to taste with salt and pepper.
7. Split scones and sandwich together with watercress butter.

39

## RAINBOW SANDWICHES
*Makes 12*

### Egg and tomato filling
3 standard eggs
3 × 15ml spoons (3 tablespoons) milk
Salt and pepper
12½g (½oz) butter
2 × 5ml spoons (1 rounded teaspoon) tomato purée

### Savoury kipper filling
1 (175g: 7oz) can kipper fillets
75g (3oz) butter
1 × 10ml spoon (1 dessertspoon) chopped parsley
Salt and pepper
1 small loaf sliced white bread
1 small loaf sliced brown bread

1. Make egg and tomato filling. Break eggs into a basin and add milk and seasonings; beat well together. Melt butter in a small pan, add eggs and scramble lightly. Stir in tomato purée, then transfer to a bowl. Leave to cool.
2. Make savoury kipper filling. Remove skin from kipper fillets and flake with a fork. Place kipper, softened butter and parsley in a bowl and mix together. Season to taste with salt and pepper.
3. Remove crusts from 12 slices of white and 12 slices of brown bread. Place 4 white and 4 brown slices on a board. Spread with egg and tomato filling. Cover white slices with brown and brown with white slices. Spread with savoury kipper filling. Top with remaining slices of bread, alternating brown and white. Cut each sandwich into 3, lengthwise.

## PIGS IN BLANKETS
*Makes 12*

12 sausages
Cooking fat
12 small slices bread
1 small 75g (2¾oz) jar meat paste
50g (1½oz) butter
Salt and pepper

1. Gently fry sausages in fat for 10 to 15 minutes, turning until evenly browned. Drain on kitchen paper and leave to cool.
2. Remove crusts from bread to make slices square. Place meat paste and softened butter in a bowl and mix together. Season to taste with salt and pepper.
3. Spread mixture evenly on bread. Place a sausage across a corner of each slice of bread and roll up (the sausage should show at each end). Secure with a cocktail stick.

*Note:* These can be made in advance and covered with kitchen foil.

## GOLDEN MEN
*Makes 12*

12 slices medium-thick bread
100g (4oz) butter
1 × 2·5ml spoon (½ level teaspoon) yeast extract
Cream cheese (or butter)

1. Prepare a moderately hot oven (200 deg C, 400 deg F, Gas Mark 6).
2. Place a gingerbread-man cutter on each slice of bread and cut round with a small knife.
3. Melt butter and yeast extract in a small pan; stir until mixed.
4. Place 'men' on a baking sheet. Brush each with butter mixture, turn over and brush other side.
5. Bake in centre of oven for 10 to 12 minutes until crisp and golden-brown. Remove from oven and cool on a wire rack.
6. Place a little cream cheese or butter in a greaseproof paper piping bag. Snip off end and pipe 'eyes', 'mouth' and 'buttons' on each 'man'.

Right: *An individual food box for children's parties, containing one Savoury raft, two Rainbow sandwiches, a Pig in a blanket, one Cheese and watercress triangle, two Golden men, a Magic toadstool, crisps, one Fruit kebab cake and a Fruit jelly.*

## SAVOURY RAFTS

### Pastry
150g (6oz) plain flour
Pinch of salt
75g (3oz) mixed cooking fats
Cold water to mix

### Filling
2 (65g: 2½oz) packets cheese and shrimp spread
3 small, firm tomatoes.

1. Prepare a hot oven (220 deg C, 425 deg F, Gas Mark 7).
2. Sift flour and salt into a bowl.

Add fats, cut into small pieces, and rub in with the fingertips, until mixture resembles fine breadcrumbs. Add sufficient water to make a firm dough.

**3.** Roll out pastry and cut into 12 circles with a 7·5cm (3in) plain cutter. Press into tartlet tins and prick all over with a fork.

**4.** Bake in centre of oven for 8 to 10 minutes. Leave until cold.

**5.** Fill pastry cases with cheese and shrimp spread. Cut tomatoes into quarters and remove seeds; spear on to cocktail sticks. Place one in the centre of each pastry 'raft' to form a 'sail'.

# FRUIT KEBAB CAKES

1 (400g: 14oz) can stoneless red cherries
1 (450g: 1lb) can pineapple cubes
1 (275g: 11oz) can mandarin oranges
100g ($\frac{1}{4}$lb) small green grapes
24 cocktail sticks
12 cup cakes

**1.** Drain canned fruit (reserve syrup for Fruit Jellies). Wash grapes and remove from stalks.

**2.** Arrange a cherry, pineapple cube, mandarin slice and grape on each cocktail stick (reserve remaining fruit).

**3.** Stick two fruit kebabs into each cup cake.

Above: *One of a child's happiest occasions – her birthday party.* (Spectrum Colour Library)

# FRUIT JELLIES
*Makes 12*

1 packet orange flavour jelly
Fruit syrup (see above)
Water
Remaining fruit from Fruit Kebabs recipe
12 waxed paper jelly cases (or 12 bowls)

**1.** Make up jelly with fruit syrup and water; leave to cool.

**2.** Place fruit in the bottom of each jelly case. Fill with jelly and leave to set.

# APPLE FIZZ
*Makes 12 glasses*

3 (500ml: 19 fluid oz) bottles apple juice
Soda water

**1.** Chill apple juice.

**2.** Divide apple juice between 12 plastic tumblers.

**3.** Top up each tumbler with soda water. Serve with straws.

# KAKO THE CLOWN

**Cake**
150g (6oz) best-quality margarine
150g (6oz) castor sugar
3 large eggs
150g (6oz) self-raising flour
$1\frac{1}{2}$ × 5ml spoons ($1\frac{1}{2}$ level teaspoons) baking powder

**Decoration**
450g (1lb) marzipan
Red food colouring
Icing sugar
4 × 15ml spoons (4 level tablespoons) warm apricot jam
1 round 18cm (7in) silver cake board
9cm ($3\frac{1}{2}$in) diameter semi-circle of red paper
Adhesive
A few coloured chocolate beans
Red candles

**1.** Prepare a cool oven (170 deg C, 325 deg F, Gas Mark 3). Grease a 750ml ($1\frac{1}{2}$-pint) and a 250ml ($\frac{1}{2}$-pint) pudding basin.

**2.** Put all cake ingredients in a large mixing bowl and beat with a wooden spoon for 1 to 2 minutes, until mixture is well blended.

**3.** Place two-thirds of mixture into the 750ml ($1\frac{1}{2}$-pint) basin and remainder in 250ml ($\frac{1}{2}$-pint) basin. Place basins on a baking sheet.

**4.** Bake in centre of oven for 35 to 40 minutes for small cake, and about 1 hour for large cake. If cooked, cakes should have stopped bubbling and should have begun to shrink from sides of basin. Press in centre with fingers and cake should spring back. Cool cakes in basins for 5 minutes, then turn out and leave to cool on a wire rack.

**5.** Weigh 75g (3oz) of the marzipan, add a few drops of red colouring and knead until evenly coloured. Make three small red 'pompoms'. Roll out remaining red marzipan to a circle, 11·5cm (4½in) in diameter, and flute edge to make a 'ruff'.

**6.** Make three small yellow marzipan pompoms.

**7.** Dust the insides of both pudding basins with icing sugar. Cut off two-thirds of remaining marzipan, place in the 750ml (1½-pint) basin and put the remaining piece in the 250ml (½-pint) basin. Press out marzipan against sides to line basins to within 2·5cm (1in) of tops for height to which cakes have risen.

**8.** Brush marzipan with warm apricot jam and press larger cake inside large basin. Using a round-bladed knife, carefully loosen around marzipan and turn cake on to cake board. Place 'ruff' in position on top of cake (see diagram).

**9.** Trim edges of smaller cake to form a ball shape and repeat method of covering with marzipan as above. Turn 'head' out on to ruff.

**10.** Roll red paper semi-circle into a cone hat and glue join with adhesive. Stick yellow pompoms on hat with adhesive and leave until firm, then place hat on head. Cut two yellow and two chocolate-coloured beans in halves, and, using apricot jam, stick one yellow half and one chocolate half together to form each 'eye' and fix to head. Stick on a red bean for 'mouth'. Using apricot jam, fix red pompoms on body of clown. Place candles in marzipan or Plasticine on cake board around base of clown.

*Note :* Cakes should be made the day before covering with marzipan. Large cake can be split twice and sandwiched with jam, if liked.

## BUTTERFLY CAKE

Above: *Butterfly cake and (back) Kako the clown.* (Paul Williams)

### Cake

100g (4oz) best-quality margarine
100g (4oz) castor sugar
2 standard eggs
100g (4oz) self-raising flour
1 × 5ml spoon (1 teaspoon) . . baking powder

### Butter Icing

150g (6oz) icing sugar
75g (3oz) butter
2 × 15ml spoons (2 tablespoons) orange juice
Yellow food colouring
1 round 20·5cm (8in) silver cake board
1 (260g: 10½oz) box of orange and lemon jelly sweets
1 chocolate-covered fudge bar
Angelica

**1.** Prepare a moderate oven (180 deg C, 350 deg F, Gas Mark 4).

Grease a 20·5cm (8in) sandwich tin and line the bottom with greaseproof paper. Brush with oil or melted fat.

**2.** Put margarine, sugar, eggs, flour and baking powder into a bowl. Mix together with a wooden spoon for 1 to 2 minutes, until well blended. Spread mixture into sandwich tin.

**3.** Bake in centre of oven for about 30 minutes. If cooked, cake should have stopped bubbling and have shrunk slightly from sides. Press in centre with fingers and cake should spring back. Cool in tin for 5 minutes, then turn out, remove paper and leave to cool on a wire rack.

**4.** Sieve icing sugar. Beat butter and icing sugar together until light and fluffy. Add orange juice and a few drops of yellow colouring and beat until smooth.

**5.** Cut cake in half to make two semi-circular cakes (see diagram 1). Spread butter icing on top and sides of each half. Place halves on cake board, rounded edges inside, to form 'wings' (diagram 2).

**6.** Cut orange and lemon sweets in halves. Arrange in alternate rows, cut sides downwards on wings, starting from outside edges and working towards centre. Keep orange jelly sweet from centre of box aside.

**7.** Place chocolate-covered fudge bar along join of wings to form the 'body'. Fix orange jelly sweet with a little butter cream at one end of body to form 'head' (diagram 3).

**8.** Cut angelica into two 4cm (1½in) thin strips and 8 'leaves'. Place strips on head to form 'antennae'. Arrange leaves along edges of wings.

## FORT WILLIAM

### Cake
100g (4oz) margarine
100g (4oz) castor sugar
2 standard eggs
100g (4oz) self-raising flour
1 × 5ml spoon (1 level teaspoon) baking powder

### Frosting
150g (6oz) icing sugar
50g (2oz) butter
50g (2oz) moist brown sugar (dark)
1½ × 15ml spoons (1½ tablespoons) milk

### Decoration
25g (1oz) desiccated coconut
Green food colouring
1 × 15ml spoon (1 level tablespoon) golden syrup or apricot jam
1 (23cm: 9in) square silver cake board

4 mini milk chocolate rolls
1 (175g: 7oz) packet milk chocolate finger biscuits
6 'soldier' candle holders with candles
4 small paper flags on cocktail sticks

**1.** Prepare a moderate oven (180 deg C, 350 deg F, Gas Mark 4). Brush a 28cm by 18cm (11in by 11in), 4cm (1½in) deep tin with melted fat or oil. Line base of tin with greaseproof paper; grease paper.

**2.** Place margarine, castor sugar, eggs, flour and baking powder into a bowl. Mix together with a wooden spoon; beat for 1 to 2 minutes.

**3.** Spread mixture in tin; level top with back of spoon. Bake in

*Below: Fort William cake.*

centre of oven for 30 to 35 minutes. Test by pressing with the fingers. If cooked, cake should spring back and have begun to shrink from sides of tin. Leave to cool in tin for 5 minutes. Loosen edges with a round-ended knife, turn out, remove paper and leave to cool completely on a wire rack.

4. Make frosting: sieve icing sugar into a bowl. Place butter, brown sugar and milk in a medium-sized saucepan over a low heat. Stir with a wooden spoon, until sugar has dissolved. Stir into icing sugar; beat until smooth.

5. Cut cake in half horizontally. Spread a little frosting over base; place other half on top. Spread frosting all over cake; mark in lines with a round-ended knife.

6. Place coconut in a small basin; add a few drops of green food colouring. Mix together until evenly coloured.

7. Spread warmed syrup or jam over cake board; sprinkle with coconut.

8. Place cake in centre of cake board; place a chocolate roll up-right at each corner. Press chocolate finger biscuits upright into icing on back and sides of cake. Cut 2 biscuits in halves; place 3 halves, with tops level with other biscuits, on front of 'fort', leaving a space for 'door'. Fill in either side of door with biscuits.

9. Arrange 5 'soldier' candle holders in position on top of cake and one on cake board in front of door. Fit candles into holders. Place a coloured paper flag on each chocolate roll.

---

## ICED ANIMAL BISCUITS
*Makes 24*

---

125g (5oz) plain flour
25g (1oz) cornflour
75g (3oz) margarine
1 × 2·5ml spoon ($\frac{1}{2}$ level teaspoon) baking powder
75g (3oz) castor sugar
1 × 15ml spoon (1 tablespoon) milk
1 egg yolk
1 × 5ml spoon (1 teaspoon) vanilla essence

**Icing**
150g (6oz) icing sugar
1 egg white
Red, yellow and green food colouring

1. Prepare a moderately hot oven (200 deg C, 400 deg F, Gas Mark 6). Lightly grease 2 baking sheets with melted fat or oil.

2. Place flour and cornflour in a bowl. Add margarine, cut into small pieces, and rub in with the fingertips, until mixture resembles fine breadcrumbs. Stir in baking powder and castor sugar.

3. Beat milk, egg yolk and vanilla essence together; add to bowl and mix with a fork to form a firm dough.

4. Turn out on to a lightly-floured board and knead until smooth. Roll out to a 3mm ($\frac{1}{8}$in) thickness. Using animal-shaped cutters, cut out 24 biscuits.

5. Using a palette knife, gently lift on to baking sheets. Bake in centre of oven for 5 to 8 minutes, until biscuits are pale golden brown at edges. Leave to cool on baking sheets for 5 minutes. Remove and leave to cool completely on a wire rack.

6. To make icing: sieve icing sugar. Place egg white in a clean, grease-free bowl. Add sufficient icing sugar to mix to consistency of thick cream.

7. Beat with a wooden spoon for 10 to 15 minutes, until icing stands up in stiff peaks.

8. Divide icing into 3 portions; colour each with a different food colouring.

9. Place each portion of icing into a greaseproof paper piping bag. Snip off end of bag just before using and outline each biscuit with a line of icing. Pipe 'eyes' with beads of icing; leave to dry. Pack, in layers, in a flat container; separate layers with greaseproof paper.

Left: *Blowing out the candles.* (Spectrum Colour Library)

Right: *Most people enjoy doing their own cooking at barbecues.* (ZEFA)

# Coming of Age

A barbecue party is an ideal way of entertaining for teenagers. Out of doors, it doesn't matter if things get spilt, and the youngsters will enjoy doing most of the cooking themselves. But do warn the neighbours if you are intending to have this type of party, as noise carries at night.

If the weather suddenly turns wet; don't despair—all our barbecue party food can be cooked under a conventional grill or in the oven, and is ideal for casual winter parties, too.

If the party is to celebrate the coming of age of either an 18 or 21-year-old, the cake, a few bottles of sparkling wine, to drink a toast, and one or two desserts can be laid out in a large room in the house.

For a large party, keep the food simple — frankfurters, hamburgers, sausages and lamb cutlets all take on a new flavour when cooked over an open fire and brushed with barbecue sauce. Chicken joints are delicious, but take quite a time to cook, so precook them in the kitchen earlier in the day, chill them quickly, then heat through on the barbecue, brushing them with the sauce from time to time.

For successful cooking, the charcoal or wood fire should be really hot before you start: light it at least 45 minutes before you intend to commence cooking. Wear oven gloves when turning the food; metal tongs are easier to use than a fork. Have a bucket of sand or water handy, in case of accidents. When the sun goes down, it often feels chilly, so mugs of hot soup will be appreciated by the guests while the main course is being cooked. Jacket potatoes and corn-on-the-cob can be cooked in the embers of the fire while the meat is being grilled on the rack.

When the meat has been cooked, use the remaining embers to grill bananas or apples, which are delicious served with cinnamon butter. Alternatively, give each guest a freshly-cut stick and some marshmallows to toast. Make sure the sticks are not dry, or the marshmallows will be lost if they catch fire!

## BARBECUED CHICKEN JOINTS

Chicken joints
Salt and pepper
Barbecue Sauce (see recipe)

1. Place chicken joints in a large saucepan; sprinkle with some salt and pepper and add ½ pint water.
2. Bring to boil, cover and simmer for 15 to 20 minutes, depending on size; drain and leave to cool.
3. Grease grill rack. Brush chicken joints with Barbecue Sauce; place on rack over hot embers of a wood fire or barbecue charcoal; grill until brown on one side. Turn over, brush with sauce and brown on other side. Serve hot.

*Note :* For a party, as finger food, use chicken leg joints and cut each joint in half.

## TOASTED CHEESE SANDWICHES
*For 4 portions*

1 packet (4) processed cheese
  slices
8 slices white bread from a large
  loaf
Softened butter

1. Place slices of cheese on 4 slices of bread; cover with remaining slices and press together firmly. Trim crusts.
2. Spread butter on outsides of each sandwich.
3. Grill on rack over hot embers of a wood fire or barbecue charcoal, until golden brown on one side, then turn and grill on other side. Serve immediately.

## LIVER AND BACON KEBABS
*For 4 portions*

250g (½lb) lambs' liver
250g (½lb) streaky bacon
Barbecue Sauce (see recipe)

1. Wipe liver and dry on kitchen paper. Cut into strips, 1in wide and 5cm (2in) long, removing gristle.
2. Remove rind and bone from bacon; cut rashers in halves horizontally.
3. Place a strip of liver on each piece of bacon and roll up; place on a skewer. Repeat with remaining liver and bacon, dividing meat between 4 skewers. Brush with Barbecue Sauce.
4. Grease grill rack. Grill kebabs over hot embers of a wood fire or barbecue charcoal, turning once, until liver is cooked, about 12 to 15 minutes. Serve immediately.

## FISH STEAKS IN FOIL
*For 4 portions*

Frozen fish steaks
Butter
Salt and pepper
Lemon juice

*Below: Liver and bacon kebabs and (back) Fish steaks in foil. (Paul Williams)*

1. Place each cod steak in a piece of freezer foil (or double thickness of ordinary foil). Dot each steak with butter, sprinkle with a little salt and pepper and add a squeeze of lemon juice.
2. Fold the foil around steaks securely; place on grill rack over embers of a wood fire or barbecue charcoal. Cook for 20 to 25 minutes. Serve hot.

## MARINADE FOR GRILLED MEAT AND FISH

1 small onion
4×15ml spoons (4 tablespoons)
  wine, cider or tarragon vinegar
8×15ml spoons (8 tablespoons)
  oil
1×5ml spoon (1 level teaspoon)
  salt
1×2·5ml spoon (½ level teaspoon)
  pepper
1×15ml spoon (1 level tablespoon)
  chopped parsley
1×2·5ml spoon (½ level teaspoon)
  mixed dried herbs

1. Peel and very finely chop onion; place in a basin. Add the remaining ingredients and mix well.
2. Leave meat or fish in marinade for several hours before cooking on a barbecue grill.

## JACKET POTATOES

Scrub and prick medium-sized potatoes; wrap in small pieces of double-thickness foil. Place in hot embers of a wood fire or barbecue charcoal and cook, turning once, until soft, for 30 to 45 minutes.

## BARBECUED FRANKFURTERS
*Makes 8*

1 packet of frankfurters
Barbecue Sauce (see recipe)
8 long, soft rolls

1. Grease grill rack. Brush frankfurters with Barbecue Sauce; grill over hot embers of a wood fire or barbecue charcoal, until lightly browned, brushing them occasionally with sauce.
2. Serve immediately in rolls, which have been warmed by the fire, with mustard or pickle.

## CHEESY FRENCH LOAF

1 small French loaf
75g (3oz) Cheddar cheese, in one piece

1. Make 8 diagonal cuts in loaf to, but not through, bottom crust.
2. Cut cheese into 8 slices, each 5cm (2in) square. Place a square in each cut.
3. Wrap loaf in a double thickness of foil; place in hot embers of a wood fire or barbecue charcoal until heated through and cheese has begun to melt. Serve hot.

Above: *At the back, Corn-on-the-cob, Cheesy French loaf and Jacket potatoes. Then Grilled bananas, Barbecued frankfurters, Barbecued chicken joints, and Barbecued lamb cutlets, with Barbecue sauce and Cinnamon butter in the foreground.*

## BARBECUED LAMB CUTLETS

Lamb cutlets
Barbecue Sauce (see recipe on page 48)

1. Grease grill rack. Trim lamb cutlets; remove excess skin and fat. Cut all fat, from end of bone, for about 1in. Cover bone with a small piece of foil.
2. Brush cutlets with Barbecue Sauce; place on grill rack over hot embers of a wood fire or barbecue charcoal. Grill for about 10 minutes, turn over, brush with sauce and grill on other side until meat is tender. Serve immediately.

## BARBECUE SAUCE

1 small onion
3 × 15ml spoons (3 tablespoons)
    oil
1 × 15ml spoon (1 tablespoon)
    vinegar
2 × 15ml spoons (2 tablespoons)
    Worcestershire sauce
125ml (¼ pint) tomato ketchup

1. Peel and finely chop onion.
2. Place all ingredients in a small saucepan; bring to boil. Cover and simmer very slowly for 10 minutes, stirring occasionally. Leave to cool. Brush over meat or vegetables while cooking on a barbecue grill.

## CHEESY HAMBURGERS
*Makes 6*

½kg (1lb) lean minced beef
1 level tablespoon chopped
    parsley
Salt and pepper
1 egg
About 100g (4oz) Cheddar cheese,
    in one piece
6 hamburger rolls

1. Grease grill rack. Place minced beef in a basin; add parsley, some salt and pepper and egg. Mix well.
2. Turn out on to a floured board; cut into 12 equal pieces. Cut cheese into 6 slices, each about 2·5cm (1in) square.
3. Form 6 pieces of meat into rounds, each 7·5cm (3in) in diameter; place a piece of cheese on each. Top with remaining pieces of meat; press out, to enclose cheese. Press edges of meat together firmly.
4. Place on grill rack over hot embers of a wood fire or barbecue charcoal.; grill for 10 minutes. Turn and grill on other side, until browned and meat is cooked through. Serve each hamburger in a roll that has been warmed at edge of the fire.

Right: *Cheesy hamburger and (back)*
*Chicken pilau.* (Paul Williams)

## CORN-ON-THE-COB

Remove husks and silk from corn. Place corn in a bowl of salted water for about 30 minutes; drain well. Brush corn with softened butter; sprinkle with a little salt and pepper. Wrap each cob securely in a piece of double-thickness foil; twist ends firmly. Place in embers of a wood fire or barbecue charcoal, or on grill of barbecue, and cook for 10 to 15 minutes, turning once.

## SAVOURY BEEF ROUND
*For 4 portions*

1 small onion
½kg (1lb) minced beef
1 × 2·5ml spoon (½ level teaspoon)
    mixed dried herbs
1 × 15ml spoon (1 level tablespoon)
    finely-chopped parsley
1 egg
1 clove of garlic (optional)

1. Grease grill rack. Peel and finely chop onion.
2. Place onion, beef, mixed dried herbs, parsley and egg into a bowl; mix well.
3. Turn out on to a floured board; form into a round cake, about 1in thick. Place on a piece of foil, invert on to grill rack, then remove foil. Place over hot embers of a wood fire or barbecue charcoal; grill until brown on underside.
4. Turn over with a fish slice; brown on other side. If desired, coarsely chop clove of garlic and sprinkle over embers to impart a slight garlic flavour to meat.
5. Serve round immediately, cut into wedges.

Right: *Barbecued kebabs and (back)*
*Savoury beef round.* (Paul Williams)

## CHICKEN PILAU
*For 8 portions*

8 cardamoms
12 cloves
12 peppercorns
8 chicken joints
8 level tablespoons desiccated
 coconut
Boiling water
½kg (1lb) long-grain rice
4 medium-sized onions
2 cloves of garlic
Salt
50g (2oz) margarine
Pinch of ground cinnamon
100g (4oz) sultanas
Chopped parsley

1. Break outer shell of cardamoms and remove seeds; discard shells. Place cardamom seeds, cloves and peppercorns in a small bowl; crush with the end of a wooden rolling pin.
2. Place spices in a large saucepan, with chicken joints; cover with 1 litre (2 pints) water. Bring to boil; cover and simmer for 35 to 40 minutes, until chicken joints are tender. Lift out chicken joints and leave to cool. Skim any excess fat from top of stock. Measure 1 litre (2 pints) stock and reserve. Wash and dry saucepan. Remove skin and bone from chicken joints; cut meat into small pieces.
3. Place coconut in a jug and add 570ml (1 pint) boiling water. Leave for 15 minutes; strain, reserving liquor. Place rice in a sieve and wash thoroughly; drain.
4. Peel and slice onions lengthwise. Peel cloves of garlic and place on a saucer with 2 × 5ml spoons (2 level teaspoons) salt. Using a round-ended knife, rub salt against garlic to crush cloves.
5. Melt margarine in saucepan; add onions and fry until golden brown, about 5 minutes. Add rice and cook for 1 minute. Add spiced stock, cinnamon, 1 level teaspoon salt and coconut liquor. Bring to boil, cover and simmer for 12 to 15 minutes, stirring occasionally, until rice is tender and stock is absorbed.
6. Add chicken pieces and sultanas; cook, stirring continuously, for a further 5 minutes. Taste and add more salt, if necessary.
7. Arrange on a warmed serving dish. Serve, sprinkled with a little chopped parsley.

## BARBECUED KEBABS
*For 4 portions*

½kg (1lb) rump steak
Marinade (see recipe)
2 small onions
1 small green pepper
100g (4oz) button mushrooms
4 small tomatoes

1. Place steak on a board and remove all fat. Beat with a rolling pin; cut into strips, each about 2·5cm (1in) wide and 7·5cm (3in) long.
2. Place pieces of steak in a basin; pour over marinade. Leave in a cool place for at least 3 hours.
3. Peel onions, being careful not to cut off root ends. Place in a saucepan, cover with cold water and bring to boil. Simmer for 5 minutes, drain, then rinse with cold water; cut into quarters.
4. Wash green pepper and cut into oblongs, 2·5cm by 3cm (1in by 1½in), discarding seeds, core and white pith. Wash and trim mushrooms. Wash tomatoes.
5. Thread meat on to 4 skewers, alternating pieces of meat with an onion quarter. Alternate green pepper and mushrooms on 4 more skewers; place a tomato on end of each skewer. Brush grill rack with a little oil.
6. Brush all skewers with marinade. Place on grill rack over hot embers of a wood fire or barbecue charcoal; grill for 10 to 15 minutes, turning once, brushing with a little marinade occasionally. Serve immediately with a green salad and Jacket Potatoes (see recipe).

## LEMON AND GRAPE TORTE

*For 8 portions*

### Base

1 (8oz) packet of digestive biscuits
2 × 15ml spoons (2 level tablespoons) golden syrup
50g (2oz) butter or margarine

### Topping

1 large can evaporated milk
1 lemon flavour jelly
Boiling water
1 lemon

### Decoration

100g (¼lb) black and green grapes, mixed
1 small carton double cream
1 × 15ml spoon (1 tablespoon) top of the milk

1. Place biscuits between 2 sheets of greaseproof paper; crush with a rolling pin.
2. Measure golden syrup carefully, levelling off spoon with a knife and making sure there is none on underside of spoon; place in a saucepan.
3. Add butter or margarine; heat until melted. Remove from heat and stir in crushed biscuits. Press mixture on to base of a deep, round, loose-based 20·5cm (8½in) cake tin.
4. Place can of evaporated milk in a medium-sized saucepan and cover with boiling water; boil for 15 minutes. Remove from pan; leave to cool for 5 minutes. Cover top of can with a cloth or piece of kitchen paper, then open can carefully and pour milk into a bowl.
5. Place jelly in a measuring jug and make up to 250ml (½ pint) with boiling water; stir until jelly has dissolved. Scrub lemon; grate rind and squeeze juice. Add to the jelly.
6. Stir jelly into evaporated milk and mix well. (It may have a curdled appearance, but this does not matter.) Leave in a cool place until on the point of setting.
7. Whisk until the mixture has doubled in volume and is thick and creamy. Pour into cake tin; leave in a cool place until set.
8. Using a wetted, round-ended knife, carefully loosen topping from side of tin. Place the tin on a 1lb-size can and gently pull cake tin down from torte. Remove torte and gently ease off base with a palette knife. Place torte on a serving dish.
9. Wash grapes; halve, then remove pips. Place cream and milk in a basin and whisk until cream just holds its shape. Place in a piping bag fitted with a large star tube.
10. Using a knife, mark top of torte into 8 sections. Pipe 'stars' of cream along marked lines.
11. Arrange a row of 3 grape halves in each section, alternating black and green grapes, around torte (see picture). Pipe a row of stars around top edge of torte. Keep in a cool place.

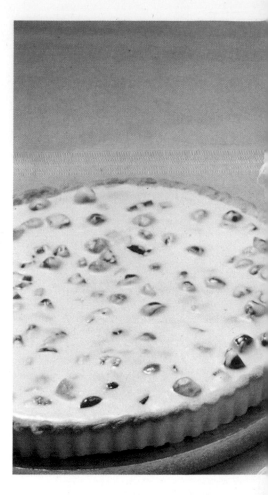

## GLACÉ ALMOND FLAN

*For 10 to 12 portions*

### French Flan Pastry

250g (10oz) plain flour
100g (4oz) castor sugar
150g (6oz) butter or margarine
2 egg yolks

### Filling

100g (4oz) castor sugar
100g (4oz) butter or margarine
2 eggs
A few drops of almond essence
50g (2oz) ground almonds
Grated rind of 1 lemon
50g (2oz) self-raising flour
6 × 15ml spoons (6 level tablespoons) raspberry jam

### Decoration

100g (4oz) yellow and red glacé cherries
25g (1oz) angelica
200g (8oz) icing sugar
Juice of 1 lemon

1. Sift plain flour on to a board and make a 'well' in centre; add 100g (4oz) sugar. Cut 150g (6oz) butter or margarine into small pieces and place in well, with egg yolks. Using the fingers, draw flour and sugar into butter and egg yolks, until blended. Knead pastry until smooth. Wrap in foil and leave in a cool place for at least 30 minutes, or overnight. (If left overnight, leave pastry at room temperature for about 1 hour before using.)
2. Prepare a moderate oven (190 degC, 375 degF, Gas Mark 5). Place a 28cm (11in) loose-based fluted flan tin on a baking sheet. Roll out pastry to a circle, about 28cm (11in) in diameter. Roll pastry around rolling pin and lift into flan tin. Press pastry up sides of tin and into flutes of tin. Roll off surplus pastry with rolling pin across top of flan; press into flutes again.
3. Cream 100g (4oz) sugar and 100g (4oz) butter or margarine together, until light and fluffy. Separate eggs and place whites in a clean, grease-free bowl; beat yolks into creamed mixture, with

Left: *Glacé almond flan (left) and Lemon and grape torte*

## HOT SPICED SHANDY
*Makes 8 to 10 glasses*

570ml (1 pint) pale ale
570ml (1 pint) ginger beer
1 × 2·5ml spoon (½ level teaspoon) ground cinnamon
1 × 2·5ml spoon (½ level teaspoon) grated nutmeg
Thinly pared rind of 1 lemon
50g or 75g (2oz or 3oz) soft brown sugar (light)

1. Place all the ingredients in a saucepan; heat slowly, but do not boil.
2. Strain into a warmed jug. Serve in small, warmed glasses.

## DAMPERS
*Makes 8*

200g (8oz) self-raising flour
2 × 5ml spoons (2 level teaspoons) salt
8 thick, freshly-cut sticks, each about 40cm (18in) long

1. Place flour and salt in a basin, add sufficient cold water to form a firm dough. Knead lightly.
2. Scrub ends of sticks. Divide dough into 8 equal pieces and roll each piece into a 20cm (8in) strip. Coil strips around end of sticks. Cook over hot embers of a wood fire or barbecue charcoal until lightly browned. Pull off sticks and serve immediately with butter and honey or jam.

*Note:* 150g (6oz) grated Cheddar cheese may be added to flour for Cheesy Dampers. Serve hot with butter.

## PARTY CUP
*Makes 10 to 12 glasses*

1 bottle rosé wine
3 × 15ml spoons (3 tablespoons) brandy
3 × 15ml spoons (3 tablespoons) orange squash
Orange slices
375ml (¾ pint) lemonade
Ice cubes

Mix wine, brandy and squash in a large jug. Add orange slices; leave in a cool place for 30 minutes to 1 hour. Just before serving, add lemonade and ice.

## GRILLED BANANAS
*Makes 6*

6 firm, ripe bananas

**Cinnamon butter**
50g (2oz) butter
50g (2oz) demerara sugar
1 × 5ml spoon (1 level teaspoon) ground cinnamon

1. Place bananas, in skins, on grill rack over hot embers of a wood fire or barbecue charcoal. Grill until skins turn black on underside. Turn and grill on other side, until skins turn black and the bananas feel soft.
2. Cream the butter, sugar and cinnamon together.
3. When bananas are cooked, cut skin from one side of each with a sharp-pointed knife. Serve hot, with cinnamon butter.

*Note:* Whole apples may be used; wash, core and score skins of apples; bake in foil in the embers of fire. Serve with cinnamon butter.

almond essence. Mix ground almonds, lemon rind and self-raising flour together and fold into creamed mixture. Whisk egg whites until stiff, but not dry; lightly fold into mixture.
4. Spread jam in bottom of pastry case; cover with filling. Smooth with the back of a spoon.
5. Bake in centre of oven for 30 to 35 minutes, until golden brown and firm to the touch. Leave in tin until cold. Push loose base up until flan is clear of flan tin. Remove base of tin and place flan on a large, flat serving dish or silver cake board.
6. Chop glacé cherries and angelica; sprinkle over filling in flan. Place icing sugar in a basin. Add lemon juice and stir in sufficient hot water until icing thickly coats the back of a spoon. Pour over glacé cherries and angelica in flan. Leave until set.
*Note:* If a 28cm (11in) flan tin is not available, 2 20cm (8in) fluted flan rings on baking sheets may be used.

# Happy Anniversary

We've planned delicious food for a really memorable 25th wedding anniversary party, but if you can't wait that long to try our recipes, follow our plan for your next great occasion.

Our party provides food for 12 people; you can easily multiply the quantities, if you plan to have more guests. Most of the food can be prepared in advance and needs just the last-minute touches on the day.

There are recipes for cocktail savouries to start with; serve these with sweet and dry sherry. A bottle of each is more than enough for 12 people. The main course and sweet of our buffet party supper are planned so that they can easily be eaten with a fork.

Cut the cake and drink the toasts to the celebrating couple later on in the evening. A medium-sweet sparkling wine would be ideal for the toast, if you don't wish to buy champagne.

## COCKTAIL VOL-AU-VENTS
*Makes 36*

36 frozen, cocktail size, uncooked vol-au-vent cases or 1 large packet and 1 small packet of frozen puff pastry, just thawed, or 1kg to 1¼kg (2¼ to 2½lb) home-made puff pastry
Beaten egg or milk to glaze
White sauce (see recipe)
Chicken and mushroom, shrimp and parsley, and ham fillings (see recipe)
Salt and pepper

1. Follow instructions on packet for thawing, glazing and baking vol-au-vent cases, or, if using bought or home-made puff pastry, proceed as follows: Prepare a hot oven (210 degC, 425 degF, Gas

*Left: Happy anniversary.* (Colour Library International)

Mark 7). Roll out pastry to about 6mm (¼in) thickness and cut out 36 circles with a 8·5cm (2¼in) fluted cutter. Place on baking sheets in rows of two quite close together. Using a 3cm to 3·5cm (1¼in to 1½in) plain cutter, mark centre of each vol-au-vent, without cutting right through pastry.

2. Glaze with beaten egg or milk. Place 1 baking sheet of vol-au-vents on shelf in centre of oven and 1 on shelf just above centre of oven; cook for 10 to 15 minutes, until golden brown. Repeat with remaining vol-au-vents. Leave to cool on a wire rack; press down centres of vol-au-vents.

3. To fill vol-au-vents: Place 5 × 15ml (5 level tablespoons) of white sauce in each of the three basins containing fillings; mix well. Taste and season with salt and pepper, if necessary.

4. Use each of the three fillings to fill 12 vol-au-vents, taking care to press filling well down into each one. Place vol-au-vents on a baking sheet. Cover with foil; leave in a cool place.

5. **To serve:** Prepare a very cool oven (140 degC, 275 degF, Gas Mark 1). Remove foil and heat vol-au-vents in centre of oven for about 10 minutes.

6. Garnish each chicken and mushroom vol-au-vent with a cooked slice of mushroom, each shrimp and parsley vol-au-vent with a shrimp, and each of the ham vol-au-vents with a small sprig of parsley. Place on warmed serving dishes and serve immediately.

## WHITE SAUCE

25g (1oz) margarine
25g (1oz) plain flour
250ml (½ pint) milk
1 × 2·5ml spoon (½ level teaspoon) salt
Pepper

1. Melt margarine in a small saucepan, stir in flour and cook for 2 minutes without browning.
2. Stir in milk and bring to boil, stirring; simmer for 2 minutes. Add salt and a shake of pepper, mix well and remove from heat.

## HAM FILLING

150g (6oz) cooked ham
Sprigs of parsley

Cut ham into 6mm (¼in) dice. Place ham in a basin, cover and leave in a cool place. Reserve parsley for garnish.

## SHRIMP AND PARSLEY FILLING

2 × 75g (2¾oz) jars shrimps
2 × 5ml spoons (2 level teaspoons) chopped parsley

1. Drain shrimps thoroughly. Reserve 12 shrimps for garnish.
2. Place remainder in a small basin, add chopped parsley and mix well. Cover basin and leave in a cool place.

## CHICKEN AND MUSHROOM FILLING

1 chicken leg joint (about 450g/14oz)
1 small onion
½ × 2·5ml spoon (¼ level teaspoon) salt
Pepper
50g (2oz) button mushrooms
25g (1oz) butter
2 × 5ml spoons (2 teaspoons) lemon juice

1. Wash chicken joint; cut across leg joint into 2 pieces. Place

53

chicken pieces in a saucepan.

**2.** Peel and quarter onion; add to saucepan with salt, a shake of pepper and 250ml (½ pint) water. Bring to boil, cover and simmer for about 30 minutes, until chicken is tender.

**3.** Lift chicken from stock, and leave to cool. Remove chicken meat from bones; discard bones and skin. Cut meat into small pieces. Place meat in a basin.

**4.** Wash and trim mushrooms; slice mushrooms thinly.

**5.** Melt butter in a small frying pan, add lemon juice and mushrooms and cook gently for about 5 minutes. Drain mushrooms. Reserve 12 mushroom slices for garnish and place remaining cooked mushrooms in basin with chicken. Cover basin and leave in a cool place.

## COCKTAIL OPEN SANDWICHES
*Makes 36*

### Bases
6 slices brown bread from a small
   sliced loaf
6 slices white bread from a small
   sliced loaf

### Toppings
Butter
Cheddar cheese
Cream cheese
Cooked silverside of beef
Scrambled egg
Salami slices
Cooked pork
Stilton cheese
Shrimps
Mayonnaise
Salmon and anchovy paste

### Garnishes
Radishes
Cucumber twists
Hard-boiled egg slices
Lumpfish roe
Stuffed olives
Wedges of tomato
Brisling
Spring onions
Black and green grapes
Cocktail onions
Twists and quarter-slices of lemon

**1.** Trim crusts from slices of brown and white bread; butter slices.

**2.** Cut a slice of brown bread into 3. Place a small square of Cheddar cheese in centre of each piece and a teaspoonful of cream cheese on either side. Garnish with radish quarters and twists of cucumber.

**3.** Place a thin slice of silverside on a slice of brown bread; cut into 3. Garnish with half slices of hard-boiled egg and roe.

**4.** Pile scrambled egg on a slice of brown bread; cut into 3. Garnish with radish quarters and roe.

**5.** Spread a slice of brown bread with cream cheese; cut into 3 and top each with a salami cornet. To make salami cornets; remove skin from salami slices and roll each firmly into a cornet shape. Place a little cream cheese into each cornet; garnish with sliced, stuffed olives.

**6.** Place a thin slice of pork on a slice of brown bread; cut into 3. Place a teaspoonful of cream cheese on top of each; garnish with tomato wedges.

**7.** Pile scrambled egg on a slice of brown bread; cut into 3. Garnish with brisling and 'fanned' spring onions. (Cut the root ends of spring onions into 4; place onions into a basin of cold water and leave for 10 minutes, or until stem 'fans' out.)

**8.** Cut a slice of white bread into 3; top with salami cones and twists of cucumber. To make salami cones; remove skin from slices of salami; cut each slice through to centre. Fold around to make a cone and press firmly. Place a little cream cheese inside each cone.

**9.** Place a thin slice of Stilton cheese on a slice of White bread; cut into 3. Garnish with halved black grapes and cocktail onions.

**10.** Spread a slice of white bread with cream cheese; cut into 3. Garnish with small pieces of Stilton cheese and halved green grapes.

**11.** Cut a slice of white bread into 3.

*Right: From the back, reading clockwise:
Cocktail vol-au-vents, Quick pizza
squares, Cheese and almond savouries,
Celery boats, Cocktail open sandwiches.*

Mix 1 rounded tablespoon of drained shrimps with 2 level teaspoons mayonnaise. Pile mixture on bread; garnish with quartered slices of lemon and twists of cucumber.

**12.** Spread a slice of white bread with salmon and anchovy paste; cut into 3. Garnish with brisling and twists of lemon.

**13.** Place a thin slice of pork on a slice of white bread; cut into 3. Garnish with wedges of tomato and cucumber twists.

**14.** Place Cocktail Open Sandwiches on serving dishes; cover with self-clinging transparent plastic film. Keep in a cool place for up to 12 hours before serving.

## QUICK PIZZA SQUARES
*Makes 24*

3×15ml spoons (3 level
  tablespoons) tomato ketchup
6 processed cheese slices
1 (50g: 2oz) can anchovy fillets
12 black olives

**Scone base**
100g (4oz) self-raising flour
½×2·5ml spoon (¼ level teaspoon)
  salt
25g (1oz) margarine
4×15ml spoons (4 tablespoons)
  milk

1. Prepare a moderately hot oven
(200 degC, 400 degF, Gas Mark
6). (See note at end of recipe, if
preparing dish in advance.) Lightly
grease a shallow 28cm by 17·5cm
(11in by 7in) tin.
2. Place flour and salt in a bowl.
Add margarine, cut into small
pieces, and rub in with the fingertips until mixture resembles fine
breadcrumbs. Add milk; stir with
a fork until just mixed. Turn out
on to a floured board; knead lightly
and roll out to an oblong 28cm by
17·5cm (11in by 7in).
3. Lift dough over rolling pin and
place in tin. Press dough into
corners and trim sides, if necessary, so that base of tin is evenly
covered with dough.
4. Spread tomato ketchup evenly
over dough. Arrange cheese slices
on top, to cover ketchup.
5. Drain anchovy fillets; cut fillets
in halves lengthwise; arrange over
cheese, in a lattice pattern. Cut
each olive in half; remove stone
and place halves in centre of each
'diamond' lattice.
6. Bake in centre of oven for 10 to
15 minutes or until cheese is
golden brown. Leave to cool in tin
for 5 minutes. Cut pizza into 24
squares. Place squares on a warmed serving dish and serve while
they are warm.
*Note:* To prepare in advance,
make pizza and cover with foil.
Leave in a cool place for up to 8
hours, then bake as described
above.

## CHEESE AND ALMOND BALLS
*Makes 24*

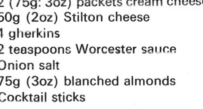

2 (75g: 3oz) packets cream cheese
50g (2oz) Stilton cheese
4 gherkins
2 teaspoons Worcester sauce
Onion salt
75g (3oz) blanched almonds
Cocktail sticks

1. Place cream cheese in a basin.
Sieve Stilton cheese into basin;
beat together until smooth.
2. Finely chop gherkins; add
gherkins, Worcester sauce and a
shake of onion salt to cheese. Mix
together; cover basin and leave in
a cool place for 15 minutes.
3. Remove rack from grill pan and
prepare a moderate grill. Chop
almonds; place in grill pan and
grill until golden brown. Place
almonds on a plate.
4. With the hands, roll cheese mixture carefully into 24 small balls,
each about 2cm (¾in) in diameter;
roll each ball in chopped almonds.
Place on a serving plate; cover with
self-clinging transparent plastic
film and keep in a cool place.
5. **To serve:** Remove plastic film
and place a cocktail stick in each
Cheese and Almond Ball.

## CELERY BOATS
*Makes about 24*

---

1 head of celery (about 9 sticks)
2 spring onions
225g (½lb) cream cheese
Salt and pepper
1×5ml spoon (1 level teaspoon)
   tomato ketchup
Paprika
6 stuffed olives

---

1. Wash celery; trim ends. Wash, trim and finely slice spring onions. Divide cream cheese equally between 2 basins.
2. Add spring onions to 1 basin; taste and season with salt and pepper. Add tomato ketchup to other basin; taste and season with salt and pepper.
3. Place onion mixture into a piping bag fitted with a 1cm (½in) plain tube. Pipe mixture into channels in half the number of celery sticks. Wash piping bag and dry thoroughly. Place tomato mixture in piping bag and pipe into remaining celery sticks.
4. Cut celery into 4cm (1½in) lengths. Sprinkle tomato-flavoured boats with a little paprika. Place 2 thin slices of stuffed olive on each spring onion-flavoured boat. Arrange on a serving dish, cover with self-clinging transparent plastic film and keep in a cool place until required.

---

## COLESLAW
*For 12 portions*

---

225g (½lb) carrots
1 medium-sized onion
1kg (2lb) white cabbage
125ml (¼ pint) thick, mild
   mayonnaise
1×15ml spoon (1 tablespoon)
   lemon juice

---

1. Scrape, wash and grate carrots. Peel and grate onion.
2. Wash cabbage and discard tough stalk and outside leaves; shred very finely. Mix mild mayonnaise and lemon juice together in a

large bowl. Add carrot, onion and cabbage; stir mixture carefully until coated with dressing.
3. Place coleslaw in a serving dish. Cover dish with foil; leave in a cool place.

---

## COLD TURKEY
*For 12 to 15 portions*

---

**Cold turkey**
1 oven-ready turkey, about 3½kg
   (7lb) drawn weight

**Stuffing**
1 large onion
100g (4oz) mushrooms
100g (4oz) streaky bacon
Lard
150g (6oz) long-grain rice
Salt and pepper
Cooked turkey liver (from giblets)
1 egg

---

1. Remove giblets from turkey; wipe inside with kitchen paper. Place giblets in a saucepan, cover with cold water and bring to boil. Cover and simmer for 1 hour. Strain; reserve stock and liver.
2. Peel and finely chop onion. Wash and chop mushrooms. Remove rind and bone from bacon; cut bacon into small dice.
3. Melt 25g (1oz) lard in a large frying pan. Add the onion, mushrooms and bacon; fry lightly. Add rice; stir over a moderate heat until fat has been absorbed.
4. Add 570ml (1 pint) giblet stock; bring to boil and gently cook, stirring occasionally, for about 20 minutes, until rice is cooked. Test by pressing a grain between finger and thumb. Taste and add salt and pepper; leave to cool.
5. Chop turkey liver. Beat egg and add to stuffing, with liver.

Above: *From the back, reading clockwise: Chocolate orange gâteau, Fresh fruit salad, Cold roast turkey, Green salad, Pasta salad, Coleslaw, Potato and sweetcorn salad.*

**6.** Prepare a moderate oven (190 degC, 375 degF, Gas Mark 5).
**7.** Calculate cooking time of turkey by adding weight of stuffing ingredients to drawn weight of bird, to find total weight. Allow 30 minutes per kg (15 minutes per lb) up to 7kg (14lb) and 20 minutes per kg (10 minutes per lb) for every kg (1lb) over 7kg (14lb).
**8.** Stuff neck end of bird. Truss turkey with fine string. Cover breast with lard. Wrap in a double thickness of greaseproof paper and tie securely with string.
**9.** Place on shelf in centre of oven and place a tin underneath to catch any drips.

**10.** When cooked, slit paper underneath turkey, to allow juices to run into tin, before removing turkey from oven. Place turkey on a wire rack. Remove paper and string; leave to cool. Place on a serving dish, remove trussing string; cover with foil or transparent film; leave in a cool place.

## FRENCH DRESSING

300ml (12 fluid oz) oil
150ml (6 fluid oz) vinegar
2 × 5ml spoons (2 level teaspoons) salt
3 × 2·5ml spoons (1½ level teaspoons) sugar
1 × 5ml spoon (1 level teaspoon) pepper
1 × 5ml spoon (1 level teaspoon) dry mustard

Place all ingredients in a small basin; beat with a fork. Alternatively, place in a small screw-topped jar or firmly-closed container; shake vigorously, or, if you have an electric liquidiser, place all the ingredients in goblet and run machine until well blended. Store in a bottle or plastic container. Shake before using.
*Note:* Dressing gives a better flavour than malt vinegar.

## GREEN SALAD
*For 12 portions*

1 bunch of spring onions
2 heads of lettuce
Half a small cucumber
2 medium-sized green peppers

**1.** Wash and finely slice spring onions. Remove and discard outer leaves from lettuce; wash lettuce well. Wash cucumber and cut into small dice.
**2.** Cut a thin slice from stem ends of peppers. Discard seeds, core and white pith; cut peppers into rings.
**3.** Pull lettuce leaves into pieces.

Mix all ingredients together in a large bowl. Cover and leave in a cool place until required. Serve with French Dressing.

## POTATO AND SWEET CORN SALAD
*For 12 portions*

2kg (4lb) potatoes
7 tablespoons French Dressing (see recipe)
1 large 300g (11½oz) can sweet corn kernels
1 small 110g (4¾oz) bottle salad cream
2 × 5ml spoons (2 level teaspoons) salt
1 × 2·5ml spoon (½ level teaspoon) pepper

**1.** Wash and peel potatoes; cut into 1cm (½in) cubes. Cook in boiling, salted water until tender. Drain, rinse in cold water and dry on kitchen paper. Place French Dressing in a bowl, add potatoes and stir lightly, to coat; leave until cold.
**2.** Drain sweet corn kernels. Stir into potato mixture with salad cream, salt and pepper; mix well. Pile into a serving dish. Cover and leave in a cool place until required.

## PASTA SALAD
*For 12 portions*

200g (8oz) quick-cooking macaroni
6 × 15ml spoons (6 tablespoons) French Dressing (see recipe)
Juice of 1 lemon
6 × 15ml spoons (6 level tablespoons) salad cream
3 eating apples
2 heads of chicory
1 (150g: 6½oz) can red peppers
75g (3oz) stuffed olives

**1.** Cook macaroni, as directed on packet. Drain in a sieve or colander; rinse with cold water and return to saucepan. Add French Dressing to pan and toss, to coat macaroni.

2. Mix lemon juice and salad cream together in a bowl. Peel, core and dice apples; place in bowl and stir mixture carefully, to coat. Wash and trim chicory; slice 1 head and add to bowl. Chop red peppers and slice olives; add to bowl, with macaroni. Stir mixture carefully until coated with dressing.

3 Pile Pasta Salad in a serving bowl. Arrange chicory spears from remaining head of chicory around edge of serving bowl. Cover, and leave in a cool place until required.

## CHOCOLATE ORANGE GATEAU
*For about 12 portions*

### Sponge
3 eggs
150g (6oz) castor sugar
4×15ml spoons (4 tablespoons) hot water
150g (6oz) plain flour
2×15ml spoons (2 level tablespoons) cocoa
2×5ml spoons (2 level teaspoons) baking powder

### Filling and decoration
150ml (6⅔ fluid oz) carton double cream
150ml (6⅔ fluid oz) carton single cream
4×15ml spoons (4 tablespoons) sherry or orange juice
50g (2oz) plain chocolate
1 (280g: 11oz) can mandarin oranges
13 orange-flavoured chocolate sticks

1. Prepare a moderate oven (190 degC, 375 degF, Gas Mark 5). Brush a deep, round 20cm (8½in) cake tin with oil or melted fat and line base and side of tin with greaseproof paper; grease paper.
2. Bring a saucepan of water to boil and remove from heat. Place eggs, sugar and hot water in a bowl and whisk over saucepan until mixture thickens and leaves a trail when whisk is lifted. Remove bowl from saucepan; whisk until cool.
3. Sift flour, cocoa and baking powder together; carefully fold into egg mixture, cutting through

mixture with a metal spoon. Pour into prepared tin and bake in centre of oven for about 35 to 40 minutes. Test by pressing with the fingers. If cooked, cake should spring back, have stopped bubbling and have begun to shrink from side of tin. Turn out, remove paper and leave to cool on a wire rack.
4. Place double and single cream in a basin and whisk until just stiff. When cool, cut cake into 3, horizontally; using a sharp knife, make 2 horizontal cuts to divide cake into three, measuring from highest point (not from top edge); cut evenly around edge, following line of both cuts; with a long knife, cut top section through to centre, turning cake, until cut is right through layer; remove top layer and cut remaining piece similarly.
5. Sprinkle bottom layer of sponge with 2 tablespoons sherry or orange juice.
6. Spread about one-fifth of cream on bottom layer. Place centre layer of sponge on top and sprinkle with remaining sherry or orange juice. Spread with another fifth of cream. Cut a 12·5cm (5in) circle out from centre of top layer of sponge, and reserve. Place outside ring of top layer on cake. Spread another fifth of cream around side of cake.
7. Coarsely grate chocolate. Hold top and bottom of cake and press side on to chocolate to coat.
8. Spread reserved circle of cake and top of cake with one-fifth cream. Dip circle in grated chocolate. Drain mandarin oranges; reserve 13 for decoration and chop remainder. Stir chopped mandarin oranges into remaining cream and pile in centre cavity of cake. Place circle on top. Arrange reserved mandarin oranges around edge of gateau. Place an orange-flavoured chocolate stick between each mandarin orange. Keep cake in a cool place until ready to serve.

## FRUIT SALAD
*For 12 portions*

3 oranges
1 (300g: 12oz) can pineapple rings
1 large 500g (15½oz) can peach slices
1 (250g: 10½oz) can cherries
225g (½lb) green grapes
225g (½lb) black grapes
450g (1lb) eating apples
Juice of 3 lemons
450g (1lb) pears
25g (1oz) granulated sugar
Boiling water
450g (1lb) bananas

1. Using a sharp or serrated knife, remove rind and pith from oranges; hold each orange over a bowl and cut out segments, discarding pith and pips. Place segments in a large bowl. Drain and add syrup from cans of pineapple rings, peach slices and cherries. Cut each pineapple ring into 8 pieces, each peach slice into 4, and each cherry into half, removing stones from cherries. Add pineapple, peaches and cherries to bowl.
2. Wash grapes, halve and remove pips; add to bowl. Peel, core and cut apples into 6mm (¼in) dice. Place in a bowl with lemon juice. Peel, core and dice pears; add to apples. Turn apples and pears in lemon juice to coat, then drain, reserving the lemon juice. Add apples and pears to fruit salad in bowl.
3. Dissolve sugar in 250ml (½ pint) boiling water; cool and add to fruit salad. Cover bowl and leave in a cool place overnight, if it is possible.
4. Just before serving, peel bananas; slice, at an angle. Toss slices in reserved lemon juice and add to fruit salad. Serve with cream.

58

# 25TH **ANNIVERSARY CAKE**

1 round 20·5cm (8in) rich fruit
  cake

**Almond Paste**
300g (12oz) ground almonds
150g (6oz) icing sugar
150g (6oz) castor sugar
Sufficient egg yolk to bind
1×2·5ml spoon ($\frac{1}{2}$ teaspoon)
  almond essence
1×5ml spoon (1 teaspoon)
  lemon juice
Apricot jam

**Royal Icing**
900g (1$\frac{1}{2}$lb) icing sugar
4 egg whites
3×2·5ml spoons (1$\frac{1}{2}$ teaspoons)
  glycerine

**Sugar Roses**
2×5ml spoons (2 level teaspoons)
  gelatine
15g ($\frac{1}{2}$oz) lard
Icing sugar
Pink food colouring

**Decoration**
1 round 25cm (10in) silver cake
  board

1m (1yd) of 2cm ($\frac{3}{4}$in) silver
  paper braid
14 silver leaves
1m (1yd) of 3cm (1$\frac{1}{4}$in) pink
  ribbon
1 silver 'happy anniversary'
  motif

---

**1.** Place ground almonds, 150g
(6oz) icing sugar and the castor
sugar in a bowl. Stir in sufficient
egg yolk, the almond essence and

lemon juice, to bind to a stiff paste. (Store egg whites in a covered jar in a cool place for use in royal icing.)

2. Knead almond paste lightly and cut in half. Roll out half on a board, well dredged with icing sugar, to a circle, 2·5cm (1in) bigger all round than top of cake. Brush with warmed, sieved apricot jam and invert cake on to almond paste. Roll over base of cake with a rolling pin, to press almond paste on to cake. Using a round-ended knife, press almond paste under cake; cut off any surplus, keeping knife pressed against side of cake. Invert cake on to an upturned plate.

3. Using a piece of string, measure around cake and cut string to exact size. Cut another piece of string to the exact height of cake. Roll out remainder of almond paste to an oblong and trim it to measure half the length of longer piece of string by twice the height of cake. Cut it in half lengthwise; brush both halves with apricot jam.

4. Hold top and bottom of cake carefully and roll side of cake on to almond paste, making sure that top and bottom edges are level. Place on an upturned plate; smooth joins with a knife. Leave for at least a day before covering cake with royal icing.

5. Sieve 900g (1½lb) icing sugar into a bowl. Place egg whites in a clean, grease-free bowl. Add sufficient icing sugar and mix to a consistency similar to that of thick cream. Beat with a wooden spoon for 10 to 15 minutes, until icing is very stiff and stands up in stiff peaks, when spoon is lifted out of bowl. Beat in glycerine. Cover bowl with a damp cloth during the whole time icing is being used, to prevent a skin forming.

6. Place a little icing in centre of cake board to secure cake; place cake centrally on board. Using a palette knife, spread some icing over top of cake, working backwards and forwards with knife to remove bubbles.

7. Use a well-scrubbed ruler to smooth icing on cake. Hold ruler at each end and steadily draw towards you. Repeat until a satisfactory surface is obtained, but keep icing free of crumbs and the bowl covered with damp cloth.

8. Spread icing on side of cake and smooth with a palette knife. Leave icing for at least 3 hours, or over night, to dry. Smooth off any rough edges with a small knife or a piece of fine emery paper. Brush off powdered sugar; ice top and side of cake with a second coat of icing. Leave for at least 12 hours to become really hard. Keep remaining icing in an air-tight container; reserve for decoration.

9. **To make sugar roses:** Measure 3 × 15ml spoons (3 tablespoons) water into a small basin; add gelatine. Place basin in a saucepan of water over a moderate heat and stir until gelatine has dissolved; stir in lard.

10. Sieve 300g (12oz) icing sugar into a bowl. Add gelatine mixture; mix well. Gradually add about 200g (8oz) sieved icing sugar until the consistency of a soft dough.

11. Turn out on to a board that has been dusted with icing sugar and knead until smooth. Cut mixture in half; knead pink food colouring into each half, making 1 half a deeper pink than the other. Keep icing wrapped in a polythene bag or in an air-tight container, to prevent drying.

12. Take out a small piece of icing and roll into a ball; shape into a tall cone. Take another small piece of icing and, using finger and thumb, press into a petal shape. Dampen petal base and wrap around cone. Repeat, making more petals and arranging them, overlapping, around cone to form a 'rose'. Place on a tray and leave to dry overnight. Make a selection of roses, in different sizes and shades of pink, for top of cake, and 4 small roses for around edge of cake. Store in an air-tight container, layering roses between sheets of soft kitchen paper.

13. Beat reserved royal icing; beat in a little sieved icing sugar until the icing stands in stiff peaks. Place in a greaseproof paper piping bag, without a piping tube. Snip off point of bag, then pipe a row of beads around top and bottom edges of cake.

14. Cut silver braid to fit around edge of cake board. Using a little royal icing, fix silver braid around edge of board. Arrange a selection of roses, to form a spray, on top of cake; fix in place with a little royal icing. Place 6 silver leaves between roses.

15. Arrange 4 small roses, each with 2 silver leaves, around edge of board; fix in place with royal icing. Cut ribbon to fit around side of cake. Place ribbon around cake and secure with 2 stainless steel pins. Place 'happy anniversary' motif on top of cake and secure with royal icing.